ENGLISH AND COMMUNICATION SKILLS FOR STUDENTS OF SCIENCE AND ENGINEERING

English and Communication Skills for Students of Science and Engineering

S P Dhanavel

Orient BlackSwan

ORIENT BLACKSWAN PRIVATE LIMITED

Registered Office
3-6-752 Himayatnagar, Hyderabad 500 029 (A.P.), India
E-mail: centraloffice@orientblackswan.com

Other Offices
Bangalore, Bhopal, Bhubaneshwar, Chennai,
Ernakulam, Guwahati, Hyderabad, Jaipur, Kolkata,
Lucknow, Mumbai, New Delhi, Patna

First Published 2009

ISBN 13: 978 81 250 3739 2

Typeset in Life BT 10/12.6 by
OSDATA, Hyderabad 500 029

Printed at
Indcom Press
Chennai 600 042

Published by
Orient Blackswan Private Limited
160 Anna Salai, Chennai 600 002
E-mail: chennai@orientblackswan.com

PREFACE

A textbook of this kind would not have been possible without the wise counsel, good will and best wishes of Anna University authorities and a number of my colleagues. First, I would like to thank the Vice-Chancellor and the Registrar of the University for their unstinted support, encouragement and permission to work on this textbook written with the view to improving the communication skills of science and engineering students. Next, my gratitude goes to the Dean, College of Engineering, and the Chairman, Faculty of Science and Humanities, Anna University, Chennai.

It is my pleasure to thank my colleagues, Dr Premalatha Rajan, Professor K. Elango, Mr P. Sadagopan, Selection Grade Lecturer, Dr T. Shrimathy Venakatalakshmi, Assistant Professor, Dr S. Soundiraraj, Assistant Professor, Dr Veena Selvam, Lecturer, Dr Stars Jasmine, Lecturer, and Ms Sujatha Priyadharshini, Lecturer, Department of Humanities and Social Sciences, Anna University, Chennai for their cooperation and moral support in all my endeavours.

No less is my pleasure in thanking the supporting staff of our department—Mr Ghouse Bhasa, Mrs Jayalakshmi, Ms Asha Catherine, Mr T. Venkatesan, and Mr P Raja Mannar—for their unconditional support in all my academic pursuits.

My deep sense of gratitude is due to Dr F. Abdul Rahim, former Professor and Head, Department of English, Annamalai University, for his abundant faith in me as a resourceful teacher for every academic purpose. He has been a great source of motivation and support in the past several years. He also spared his valuable time to go through the first and final drafts of the book and suggested many improvements.

Further, I am deeply undebted to Mr Wilfred Fernandez and Ms Gayatri Pillai, of Orient Blackswan Pvt. Ltd, who appreciated the value of this innovative book and took the efforts to see this book in print. I am also grateful to the reviewer of this book for the valuable suggestions.

Writing this book has been a great learning experience for me. I am willing to learn from my colleagues and students who will be using this book. Please direct all your comments to dhanavelsp@yahoo.co.in with ECS as subject of the book in future editions.

S. P. Dhanavel
Professor and Head
Department of English
Anna University
Chennai 600 025, India

ACKNOWLEDGEMENTS

We are grateful to the following for permission to use copyright material: Mr John Stark for 'A Few Words on TQM', Tim Radford and the *Guardian* for 'The Gods of Cosmology', INFOCOMM for the passage on platinum mining and production in unit 2, the *Businessworld* for 'Powerful Surplus', the Azim Premji Foundation for Mr Azim Premji's speech at IIM (C), Professor Guus Berkhout for his article in the *DELFT Outlook*, Vol. 24, Professor A. R. Santhakumar for 'Building Disaster-resistant Structures', Mr Anand Agarwal of Sterlite Technologies Ltd for 'Fibre Optic Transmission has Come to Stay', *The Hindu Business Line* for 'Hypersonic Flight May become a Reality' by M. Somasekar, *The Hindu* for 'A Country Like India must have a Land Use Plan' by G. Ananthakrishnan, 'Highway to Danger' by Goutam Ghosh, 'Mobile Phone Menace' by Sandhya Soman, et. al., 'Termites Teach us Thermo-regulation' by A. Srivathsan, 'Tagore's Paintings, Sculptures to be Available Online' by Marcus Dam, 'Half of Forest Areas Fire Prone' by Staff Correspondent, 'IIT, IIM among the World's Best' by Vani Doraisamy, 'Issue is Finding Employable Graduates' by Ramya Kannan, 'India in Space' by N. Gopal Raj and the NASA and the WMAP Science team for 'What is the Fate of the Universe'. Every attempt has been made to trace copyright holders for other texts used in this book but no information has been received at the time of going to press. The publishers would be grateful for information regarding copyright holders so that due acknowledgement can be made in all future editions of the book.

CONTENTS

INTRODUCTION

English and Communication Skills for Students of Science and Engineering is a coursebook for first year students pursuing undergraduate degree courses in science and engineering.

This book has been prepared with a view to providing ample scope for students to learn and practise the five communication skills—thinking, listening, speaking, reading, and writing—in English, the global language of communication. In fact, this is a book for global professionals.

The book is organised into ten units where reading and listening texts relevant to the fields of science and engineering are used as contexts to develop communication skills. Each unit has five sections with a section on each communication skill. Each section has sub-sections on interaction, word power, comprehension, oral and written communication and language activities. The 'Insight' and 'Food for Thought' sections in the book encourage students to think and reflect on the theme discussed.

English and Communication Skills for Students of Science and Engineering is primarily a learner-centred and task-based coursebook. It reflects some of the approaches in English language teaching and learning currently in practice around the world. While communication is the chief focus, soft skills have has also been incorporated. Both teachers and students will find this book a refreshing change from run-of-the-mill English coursebooks.

HOW TO USE THE BOOK

Note to the Teacher

The concept of a teacher, particularly an English language teacher, has changed tremendously over the years. The teacher instead of 'teaching' this book to the students should play the role of a facilitator in the process of learning. The teacher should state the aim of each class activity and ensure that the students participate in the activities as effectively as possible. He or she should provide explanations and additional information, where necessary, but the students must be used as the most important resource in the classroom.

Ensuring that all the students in the class do the tasks is a tough job for the teacher. To make sure the teacher may have to move around the class to check whether everybody is doing the tasks assigned.

Motivation is the key to success. It is the teacher's job to motivate the students to learn and practise communication skills. The strongest motivation for the teachers is, of course, satisfaction in doing his or her job well. He or she has to achieve the best results ensuring that communication skills develop in the students. With English becoming the global language of communication, the teacher has to bring about a real understanding, in the students, of the need to use English in their everyday life.

The book is interaction and communication-oriented. Task-based interaction must be encouraged among students for the effective development of communication skills. The teacher has to be a guide, motivator, and facilitator for the students.

Note to the Students

Gaining proficiency in English, which is a second language for us, is not an easy task. Hard work and focused practice alone will help you achieve your goal.

Mastery over English is a must in the current global business environment. This must drive you to acquire effective communication skills in English. This book provides ample opportunities for you to develop five communication skills. The familiar communication skills are listening, speaking, reading and writing (LSRW). In this book thinking is treated as the first and foremost communication skill. Without thought, the other four skills cannot be acquired or practiced. Therefore, think accurately, clearly, and deeply to perform well in all communicative contexts.

Bring your book to the class every day. Also bring a mini-dictionary to help you with your vocabulary. Listen to the teacher and pay close attention to the instructions in the book. Organise your learning as effectively as possible. Actively participate in the learning process. Listen carefully to the listening tasks in the class. Ask your teacher questions, if you have any. When you want to share something of interest to everybody, get permission from the teacher and speak up. Most importantly, enjoy communicating in English.

Support from the Author

Any support from the author, if desired by colleagues, students, and institutions using this as a course book, will be available through e-mail. Please send your queries to **dhanavelsp@yahoo.co.in**.

UNIT 1

E-WORLD

1.1 E-language: Story of the English Language

Thinking and Interaction

Discuss the following questions in pairs and share your answers with the class.

1. Why do you think it is important to speak good English?
2. Why is English considered a global language?
3. How did English become one of the languages with the largest number of words?
4. Why did English borrow words from other languages?
5. How does English dominate the electronic world?

Word Power

Match the words in column A to their meanings in column B.

	A	B
1	prior	a. renewal of interest in art and literature
2	invaders	b. persons sent to teach Christianity
3	dialect	c. a group of powerful people with money, knowledge, and special skills
4	renaissance	d. out of date
5	obsolete	e. existing or coming before in time, order or importance
6	missionaries	f. persons entering a country with armed forces to occupy it
7	elite	g. a distinct form of language used in a place or by a class of people

Reading

Read the passage and answer the questions that follow.

Did you know that English is not the original language of England? It was introduced to the island only in the mid-fifth century by three Germanic tribes. Prior to this, Celtic was the spoken dialect. This language survives even today in the Gaelic languages of Scotland and Ireland and in Welsh. When the Germanic tribes entered the British Isles, they pushed the locals into Wales, Cornwall and Scotland. The invaders were Jutes, Saxons, and Angles. The Angles were named from Engle, their land of origin. Their language was called Englisc from which the word English is derived. They spoke a mutually intelligent dialect, which slowly evolved into English, or rather, Old English. At this time, the Vikings from Scandinavia too influenced English.

The Roman invasion in the ninth century had introduced a number of Latin words. The next influence came from the Norman Conquest in 1066 A.D. The Normans were of Germanic stock. Anglo-Norman was a French dialect that had Germanic influences in addition to Latin roots.

With the Renaissance in the 14th century, a number of Greek and Latin words entered into the English vocabulary. Gradually, Old English became obsolete. There has been a change in the written script too. Earlier English was written in an alphabet called Runic. This was replaced with the present Latin alphabet which was brought from Ireland by the Christian missionaries. Modern English language began in the sixth century and like all living languages is still growing. French and Latin had always been regarded as the fashionable dialect of literature and the elite class. But English has overtaken them all.

English is quite flexible and extends hospitality to all languages. This is the reason why foreign languages have greatly influenced the English language.

(*Source*: http://www.hindu.com/yw/2007/02/16/stories/2007021600100800.htm)

Comprehension

1. What was the original language of England?
2. What happened to the original inhabitants of England?
3. What happened to the Runic alphabet?

4. What is the contribution of Christian missionaries to English?
5. What are the languages that have helped English grow?
6. Which word other than English is repeated several times in the passage?

Understanding Adverbs

Look at the words '*mutually*' and '*gradually*'. These are called adverbs and are formed with the suffix '-ly'. By adding '-ly' to an adjective, it is possible to make an adverb. An adverb provides information on 'how', 'where', 'when', etc. an action took place.

In the space provided below list three adverbs found in the passage.

1.
2.
3.

Make adverbs from the words given below.

1. knowing
2. original
3. linguistic
4. local
5. fashionable
6. intelligent
7. additional
8. present
9. extensive
10. reasonable

Insight

1. '-ly' is added to adjectives to make adverbs
2. Suitable changes in spelling are required for some words like 'reasonable'.
3. Some adverbs may not have an '-ly' ending. (For example: *next, fast, always* and *even*)
4. Some words ending with '-ly' are not adverbs. (For example: *friendly, costly* and *ugly*)

Descriptive Writing

Describe the English language in about 125 words, focusing on its uses for the world community.

1.2 E-governance

Thinking and Interaction

Discuss the following questions in pairs and share your answers with the class.

1. What is governance?
2. Give an example of conventional governance.
3. What is e-governance?
4. What do you think are the advantages of e-governance?
5. List some disadvantages of e-governance.

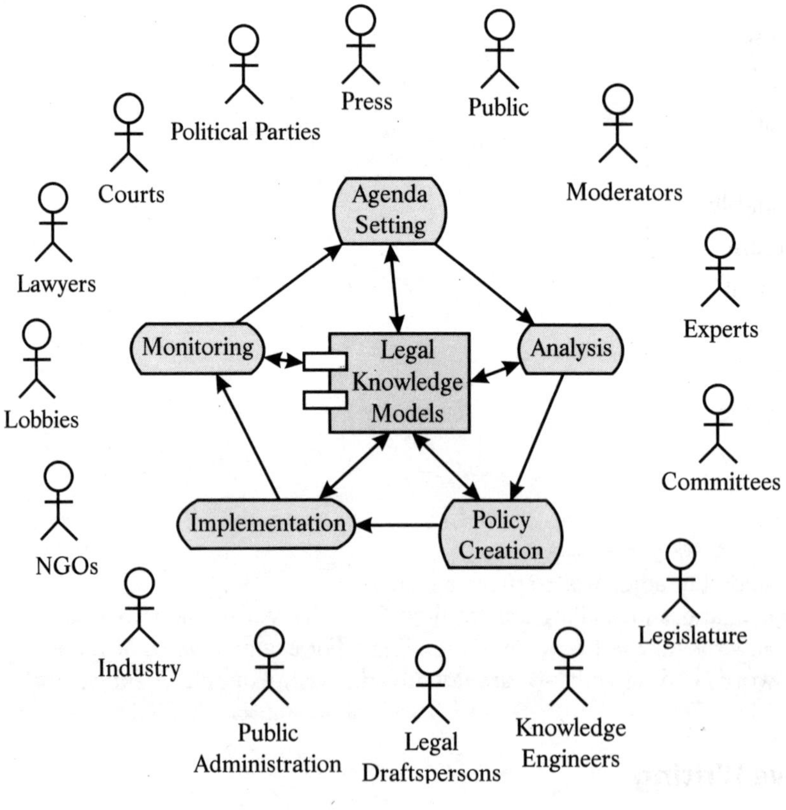

Word Power

Match the words in column A to their meanings in column B.

	A	B
1	haphazard	a. giving some identification
2	precede	b. a thing required as a condition
3	deployment	c. randomly, without any plan
4	foray	d. remarkably
5	framework	e. come or go before
6	prerequisite	f. involvement in an activity
7	tagging	g. using resources effectively
8	singularly	h. a structure giving shape and support to something

Listening

Listen to a short talk on the four stages of e-governance and fill in the blanks in the flowchart given below.

Title

↓

Stage 1

↓

Stage 2

↓

Stage 3

↓

Stage 4

Notice that the different stages of e-governance are listed sequentially using words like *firstly*, *secondly*, *thirdly*, and *lastly*. Such transitional words are very helpful in indicating progression from one stage to another.

Paragraph Writing

Write a paragraph of 125 words about the usefulness of e-governance in making India a developed country.

1.3 E-ticketing

Thinking and Interaction

Discuss the following questions in pairs and share your answers with the class.

1. How do you book your bus, railway, and air tickets?
2. What is the role of travel agents in booking tickets?
3. What are the benefits of booking your travel tickets well in advance?

Word Power

Match the words in column A to their meanings in column B.

	A	B
1	vogue	a. expected
2	slated	b. suggestion
3	passé	c. design, management, and operation of aircraft
4	reiterate	d. a current fashion
5	aviation	e. no longer fashionable
6	proposition	f. future
7	robust	g. emphasise
8	prospective	h. strong and healthy

Reading

Read the passage and answer the questions that follow.

Started by American carriers in 1994, today e-tickets are in vogue in as many as 134 countries and account for nearly 50 per cent of all air ticket sales globally. In the

US, this mode of booking is immensely popular and it commands a hefty share of 90 per cent of all tickets sold annually. Latest statistics also reveal that e-ticketing is rapidly spreading its wings in the Asia-pacific region and has finally caught up with Indian carriers too.

Recently *Indian* inked a deal with *Amadeus*, for its services operating out of Delhi, Mumbai, Bangalore, Kolkata, Chennai, and Hyderabad. E-ticketing will gradually become effective for all 300-plus flights which the airline operates on a daily basis by the end of 2007. This would be as per International Air Transportation Association (IATA) guidelines for all its affiliated airlines. With *Jet, Sahara, Air Deccan* and *Kingfisher* also offering e-ticket options, Indian aviation operators have commenced their drive for e-ticketing. And now with India's entry, this tool is likely to further expand its base. Presently, e-ticketing implementation, as far as airline bookings are concerned, stands at a low figure of 17 per cent. But the early birds in the segment like *Jet Airways* and *Air Sahara* have already started showing commendable success with e-tickets—37 and 28 per cent respectively, of their total tickets sold in the last financial year were e-tickets. And this number is only slated to get more robust in the short to medium term.

There is, however, a general misunderstanding about e-ticketing since it is often confused with any kind of online booking. But, in a practical sense, while online booking involves making use of available information on travel websites and then making a reservation, e-tickets are just the electronic avatar of an air ticket, irrespective of the source from where it has been booked. The concept paves the way for a paperless mechanism, wherein those large coupon size tickets are passé. A prospective traveller only has to book his ticket online (either through an agent or himself), take the print out, furnish it at the airport counter along with his identification card, and he will be issued a boarding pass. The check-in period gets shortened which is a major advantage of e-tickets. The information keyed in is stored in a centralised server which facilitates smooth running of the entire mechanism. To the traveller, while it eliminates the fear of loss of tickets, for agents it improves delivery costs and productivity. The biggest advantage probably is to airline companies which are likely to save as much as US $3 billion by early 2008, according to an IATA estimate.

Indian which has now decided to adopt e-ticketing in a major way (it had started this service in a limited way in 2004) calls it a major technological initiative. Says Anita Khurana, Director (Commercial), *Indian*, "This is an initiative which is very important for passenger convenience." She also finds this solution a win-win proposition for all involved. "A passenger will be able to get an e-ticket sitting in the convenience of his own house. He can take a printout and take it to the airport. And for the agents too it is a lot more convenient because they also do not need to issue a whole lot of documents and do the reports. For the airline too, it's very convenient. We don't have to keep accounts, paper reports, etc., since all records are electronically stored. So it's a win-win situation technically for all the partners and it also translates into a whole range of conveniences for passengers," she adds.

Indian officials are denying the theory that bringing in e-ticketing could well be a step to make its savings a bit bulkier. Airline operators in India will fully implement e-ticketing by the end of 2007 and are expected to save to the tune of US $200–US $300 million on an annual basis. But Khurana reiterates that this has not been the top priority of *Indian* while joining hands with *Amadeus*. "Size of the saving is very difficult for me to tell you at this juncture because once everybody comes on board and we are e-ticketing compliant in all areas, we will need to check the exact numbers. Right now, we are not looking at this initiative as a saving tool, rather we are doing it to enhance passenger convenience," she replied, when quizzed on this point. But her statements make it clear that India will definitely find a saving cushion with e-ticketing services in the long term. In the process, e-ticketing is likely to get a shot in the arm, since the push will be coming from the national carrier.

(*Source*: *Travel Trends Today,* Vol. 23, Issue no. 1, January 2007)

Comprehension

1. When was e-ticketing started?
2. Where is e-ticketing most popular?
3. Why have Indian airlines adopted e-ticketing?
4. List the various airline operators mentioned in the passage.
5. How does e-ticketing differ from online booking?
6. What is a win-win proposition?
7. Who is the main beneficiary of e-ticketing?

Gerunds and Infinitives

Look at the following sentence from the passage:

Indian officials are denying the theory that bringing in e-ticketing could well be a step to make its savings a bit bulkier.

In this sentence *'are denying'* is a verb whereas *'bringing'* is a gerund. The gerund is derived from the base verb form *'bring'* and its infinitive form is *'to bring'*. Thus, a gerund can be changed into its infinitive form and still express the meaning relevant to the context. Hence, it is possible to say,

Indian officials are denying the theory that to bring in e-ticketing could well be a step to make its savings a bit bulkier.

Where the gerund cannot be changed into its infinitive form and vice-versa without affecting the contextual meaning, it becomes a verbal noun. The difference between a gerund and a verbal noun is that a gerund retains its verb function but a verbal noun loses its verb function.

Say whether the following "–ing" words are gerunds or verbal nouns.

1. The engineer's careful drawing of the proposed administrative block saved a lot of money for the company.
2. The rapidly growing real estate business is a cause of concern for the general public.
3. Demolishing a heritage building is not allowed.
4. Metropolitan cities in India have expanded erratically due to lack of urban planning.
5. Engineering highly sophisticated designs is very easy today.

Identify the "–ing" ending words in the following sentences and replace them with infinitives.

1. Planning our national development is essential.
2. Constructing an over bridge in a heavy traffic area is easier today.
3. Nationalising rivers will help solve water disputes between different states.
4. Privatising national highways will make travel comfortable on the roads.
5. Improving infrastructure in all areas is a national priority.

Rewrite the following sentences using appropriate gerunds.

1. To visit China is one of my dreams.
2. My hobby is to play music.
3. To err is human and to forgive is divine.
4. To give and accept a bribe is unethical.
5. To waste petrol means to import more oil from other countries.

Word Origin: Greek

Look at the following words from the passage.

paper
electronic
centralised
technological
theory

These words have their origin in the Greek language. A lot of words in English are derived from Greek. For example, the root of 'technology' is '*techne*' which means 'art' or 'skill'. This root is found in words like *technical, technique, technocrat, pyrotechnic, polytechnic,* etc. 'Logy' means study. So, 'technology' means study and use of art or skill.

Using an etymological dictionary, give the root and the meaning of the following words.

	Word	**Root**	**Meaning**
1	paper		
2	electronic		
3	centralised		
4	theory		
5	predict		
6	decade		
7	crucial		
8	intelligence		
9	autonomy		
10	disposal		

Adverb Identification

Identify at least ten adverbs from the reading passage and list them in the space provided below.

	Adverbs		Adverbs
1		6	
2		7	
3		8	
4		9	
5		10	

Noun-making Suffixes

Nouns can be formed from verbs, adjectives, adverbs or from other nouns. They have certain typical endings called suffixes. Here is a list of such suffixes with examples.

Can you add a few more examples for each of the suffixes?

	Suffix	Meaning	Examples from the text	Your own examples
1	-ion	process	transportation, option, association, solution	
2	-or	person	operator, director	
3	-er	person	traveller, passenger	
4	-y	process	delivery	
5	-ity	quality	productivity, priority	
6	-ism	object, idea	mechanism	
7	-ment	state	statement, document	
8	-an	person	American, Indian	
9	-ence	state	convenience	
10	-ness	state	effectiveness	

Match the suffixes with the words and make nouns.

Here are a few examples for you.

1. manage + ment = management
2. efficient + y = efficiency
3. national + ity = nationality

	Suffix	Word	Noun
1	-ion	manage	
2	-ity	efficient	
3	-ment	national	
4	-ism	invent	
5	-ness	global	
6	-y	popular	
7	-or	natural	
8	-er	translate	

Role Play

Assume that you have an e-ticket for Delhi from Chennai. You reach the airport to catch your flight. When you check in, you find to your surprise that the airline officer refuses to give you a boarding pass because your name and ticket number are not recognised by the computer for that particular flight. Two students may assume the role of the air passenger and the airline officer and enact the scene. They must discuss the problem, and arrive at a compromise.

Food for Thought

"Governance, whether conventional or electronic, must be efficient and effective."

1.4 E-mail

Thinking and Interaction

Discuss the following questions in pairs and share your answers with the class.

1. Do you have one or more e-mail addresses?
2. How does an e-mail address differ from your postal address?
3. Who created the first e-mail service?
4. How did e-mail become such a popular form of communication?

Word Power

Match the words in column A with their meanings in column B.

	A	B
1	mail	a. to send an e-mail that you have received to someone else
2	domain	b. a computer program which can make copies of itself and is intended to prevent the computer from working normally
3	attachment	c. information stored on a computer as one unit with one name
4	forward	d. a part of the internet that belongs to a person or an organisation
5	file	e. a message or document sent over the Internet
6	virus	f. a file that you send with an e-mail message

Reading

Read the passage and answer the questions that follow. As you read the passage, underline the main points in each paragraph.

Electronic mail, or e-mail (and mail) for short, is one of the most popular uses of the Internet. Once you have an e-mail account, you can send an electronic message (like a letter) to others with e-mail accounts as long as you know their correct e-mail address.

If you have an Internet Service Provider (ISP) or commercial online service you probably already have and know your e-mail address. An e-mail address is set up like this: your username, then an @ ('at') symbol, and then a domain name (something .com, .net, or .org in most cases). For example, if you are on America Online (AOL) your e-mail address is username@aol.com, where username is your AOL screen name. Always give your full e-mail address, as in rajiv@aol.com, or mohan@yahoo.com.

Using e-mail is rather straightforward. Once you have set up an account, you just select the option that says something like "new e-mail message" or "create a new message". You'll probably be prompted with these boxes (called fields):

To:

CC:

BCC:

Subject:

Body: (sometimes the body doesn't actually say body; it's just the big area where you type your actual message.)

In the To: field you type the complete e-mail address of the person who will receive the e-mail. You may also see fields for CC: and BCC: close to your To: field. CC stands for carbon copy. If you want to send a message to multiple people, add the extra people in the CC: field (usually you separate their e-mail addresses by commas). BCC stands for blind carbon copy. BCC works just like a carbon copy, except the e-mail addresses you type in BCC do not show up to the other recipients. (Example: You send a message To: Mary and BCC: Joey. Joey will see Mary's e-mail address, but Mary won't see Joey's e-mail address because you "blinded" it by putting it in the BCC field.)

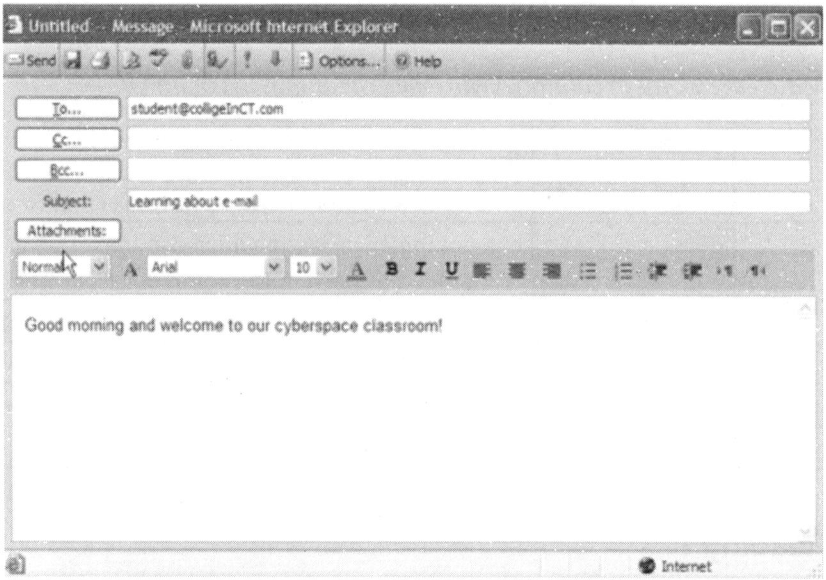

You can type anything you want as the subject and body, although the length of the subject is limited. You usually want to keep the subject to just a few words describing the content of the body of the e-mail message. You may also see options for attachments and forwards. You can add files to your e-mail by using the attachment option. You can forward (make a copy of) a message you receive from someone (if you have his or her permission, if necessary) and mail it to someone else with the forward option.

There are two things about file attachments you need to be careful of. The first thing is that you need to limit the size of the files you are sending. An attachment the size of a floppy disk (1.44MB) can take anywhere from a few seconds to a few hours for someone to receive, depending on the speed of his or her Internet connection. Get permission before sending large files to someone.

The second reason you need to be careful with attachments is that they are one of the most common ways for computer viruses to spread. As a rule you should never open an attachment from someone you don't know or don't trust. And even if you know the sender, don't open an attachment you are not expecting or an attachment that looks suspicious. Some viruses can destroy all the data on your computer, so it's best to play it safe.

CAUTION: You can also get viruses by downloading executable files (usually .com and .exe on Windows computers) from web sites. While only a very small percentage of executable files contain viruses, you still may get one. Don't download or run executable files from web sites you don't trust.

(*Source*: http://www.davesite.com/webstation/inet101/mail01.shtml)

Comprehension

1. How did the Internet become popular?
2. What is essential to send an e-mail?
3. What are the elements of an e-mail address?
4. What are the five parts of an e-mail?
5. Why should we be careful about sending and receiving attachments?

State whether the following are true or false.

1. Mail, e-mail, and electronic mail are very different uses of the Internet.
2. Even if there is a minor mistake in the receiver's e-mail address, the mail cannot be sent.
3. There is no e-mail address without the symbol @.
4. You have to fill in all fields to send a message.
5. You can send a message to any number of people through a single e-mail.
6. Addresses given in the BCC filed cannot be seen by other receivers of your mail.
7. The space for subject and body fields is unlimited.
8. There is no limit to the size of files in attachments.
9. Downloading attachments takes varying degree of time for different users.
10. All e-mails and attachments are useful and informative.

Choose the correct answer.

1. An electronic message is similar to ....
   a. a digital message

   b. a computer message
   c. a letter
   d. a technical message
2. An e-mail address has ....
   a. a user name
   b. @ symbol
   c. a domain name
   d. all the above
3. Which of the following is not a field in an e-mail?
   a. To
   b. Subject
   c. Detachment
   d. Attachment
4. A computer virus is ....
   a. a disease that affects computers
   b. a file that goes along with every e-mail
   c. a costly hardware
   d. a hidden program meant to destroy data in a computer
5. A virus can spread through ....
   a. new floppies
   b. unused compact disks
   c. trustworthy e-mails
   d. none of the above

'E' prefix

Terms like e-governance and e-commerce are commonly used. List at least five more words with e- as prefix.

1.
2.
3.
4.
5.

Noun-making Suffixes

Make nouns from the following words, using suitable suffixes.

correct	common
commercial	contain
select	suspicious
prompt	provide
complete	cautious
separate	permit
except	compute
describe	attach
destroy	

Domain Names

Internet and e-mail addresses have, what are known as, domain names. You would have come across domain names like *.com* and *.org* in some addresses. They refer to 'commerce' and 'organisation', respectively.

Find out what the following domain names indicate and write the expansions in the space provided.

Domain name	Expansion	Domain name	Expansion
.net		.tv	
.edu		.de	
.info		.in	
.mobi		.us	
.biz		.eu	

Discuss the following questions in pairs and fill in the table.

1. Why is ordinary mail known as snail mail?
2. How is e-mail effective?

Features	Snail mail	E-mail
1. definition		
2. examples		
3. advantages		
4. disadvantages		

E-mail Writing

Individually write an e-mail to your friend using the e-mail format (To, CC, BCC, Subject, Body) about how you have found e-mail more useful and effective than an ordinary mail. You may also send an e-mail about the uses of e-mail to your teacher's e-mail address using the Internet.

Food for Thought

"Today we can live without a residential address, but not without an e-mail address."

1.5 E-waste Contamination in India

Thinking and Interaction

Discuss the following questions in pairs and share your answers with the class.

1. What is waste?
2. What is e-waste?
3. What are the sources of e-waste?
4. How can you reduce e-waste?
5. What are some practicable solutions to the problem of e-waste?
6. Why is waste management a serious business today?

Word Power

Match the words in column A to their antonyms in column B.

	A	B
1	contaminating	a. production
2	hazardous	b. action
3	consumption	c. purifying
4	responsibility	d. safe
5	phase-out	e. similar
6	inaction	f. irresponsibility
7	abdicating	g. unknown
8	highlight	h. taking up one's rights
9	diverse	i. phase-in
10	known	j. conceal

Reading

Read the following passage and answer the questions that follow.

India indifferent to e-waste contamination

Some of the biggest brands in electronics industries and their suppliers are contaminating rivers and underground wells with a wide range of hazardous chemicals, according to a Greenpeace survey.

An analysis of samples taken from industrial estates in China, Mexico, the Philippines, and Thailand has revealed the release of hazardous chemicals during the manufacture of printed wiring board (PWB) and semiconductor chips, and the component assembly. The highly toxic polybrominated diphenyl ethers (PBDEs), widely used as brominated flame-retardants, are used in a wide range of processes.

India is witnessing an explosive consumption of electronic goods and equipment, and is on its way to becoming the choice destination for manufacturing.

"It is imperative that India pay heed to the alarm bells being sounded on the environmental and human health front. It is time the IT Ministry realised its responsibility to regulate the toxic impact of this industry hand in hand with promoting its growth," said Vinuta Gopal of Greenpeace India.

The study, "Cutting-Edge Contamination", was undertaken to highlight the environmental contamination resulting from manufacture of electronic equipment such as computers. Discharged wastewaters and sediments from discharge pipes/channels were analysed near PWB facilities and one component assembly facility. Where possible, treated wastewaters and treatment sludges/sediments from wastewaters and treatment plants were also collected and groundwater samples from many sites were analysed.

Evidence of environmental contamination by a diverse range of chemicals, many with known uses in this industry, was found in each of the three sectors investigated. These included both chemicals incorporated in the products and chemicals used in manufacturing processes, many with known toxicity to humans and other potential environmental impacts.

Some chemicals were found in waste streams from more than one sector, including some toxic and environmentally persistent groups such as PBDEs, phthalates used as plasticisers (softeners) in plastics, certain chlorinated solvents, and high levels of some heavy metals.

Other chemicals found in waste streams and groundwater samples were specific to each of the manufacturing sectors, for example brominated flame-retardant tetrabromo-bisphenol-A (TBBPA) and photo initiator-related chemicals at PWB manufacturing sites.

Flame-retardants are chemicals added to a wide variety of materials, including casings and components of many electronic goods. Two widely used groups of chemicals are PBDEs and TBBPAs.

(*Source*: http://www.hindu.com/2007/02/19/stories/2007021901050900.htm)

Comprehension

1. What is the purpose of this article?
2. What does the Greenpeace survey say about the problem of e-waste?
3. How does the author define fire-retardants at the end of the passage?
4. Who is the possible target audience of this passage?

Adjective-making Suffixes

Look at the following words from the text.

hazardous
industrial
explosive
electronic
environmental

These words are adjectives and they qualify the words that come after them. They are formed from words like *hazard, industry, explosion, electron,* and *environment* with the help of suffixes *-ous, -ial, -ive, -ic,* and *-al.*

Here are a few more suffixes which also make adjectives. They are given in the following table with examples. You may also add your own examples.

	Suffix	Examples	Your examples
1	-ical	technical, magical	
2	-able	memorable, reliable	
3	-ible	possible, legible	
4	-ant	abundant, significant	
5	-ent	proficient, magnificent	
6	-ful	faithful, careful	
7	-y	bulky, easy	
8	-less	tasteless, odourless	
9	-ate	considerate, moderate	
10	-ian	authoritarian, humanitarian	

Understanding Voice

Look at the underlined verbs in the passage. These verbs are in the passive voice. When writers want to give importance to the subject and not to the person, they use passive voice. It is usually found in scientific and technical writing. However, it is advisable to use active voice in all forms of writing.

Change the voice of the following sentences.

1. The table was shifted from the first floor to the ground floor.
2. The electronic industry produces a lot of waste material.
3. Domestic garbage is collected in green boxes by the municipal corporation.
4. The students have developed a new machine for segregating wastes.
5. We must keep our environment clean.

Insight

> Shifting the subject, and object in a sentence can be used to show varying degrees of emphasis, on an element. Consistent emphasis on a particular idea in the sentences in a paragraph makes the paragraph coherent and well developed.

Flowchart

Read the following passage and draw a flowchart to represent the process of recycling e-waste.

Old computers are not deleted: The electronics recycling process

The recycling process for Cathode Ray Tubes (CRTs) begins on a disassembly line. Workers remove the recyclable plastic or wooden case, metal chassis, yoke, PC board, wire and metal strap from the CRT. These materials are all sorted for individual commodity sales. The resulting CRT is a whole glass tube (spread with lead) with an internal metal frame.

The CRTs are then loaded onto a conveyor system that leads into the CRT crusher. This self-contained unit allows for easy transportation, total weather protection, dust containment and complete air filtration. The crusher can process 100–150 CRTs per hour, or over 15 tons per day.

Once the CRTs enter the crusher, they drop into a rotating hammer mill. The hammers hit the glass, causing the CRT to implode into pieces of glass and metal. A magnet pulls metal from the mix, and a screen is used to sift the glass to produce the desired size. Metals and crushed glass are separately discharged from the bottom of the system into commodity containers for shipment. The lead-contaminated glass is shipped to a primary lead smelter. The smelter uses the glass as a fluxing agent in the processing of raw lead ore. The lead from the glass becomes part of their end product, which is then sold to be used in the manufacture of products such as new CRTs, x-ray shielding, bullets and batteries.

Circuit boards are eventually ground up and smelted. The gases from this process are captured and the resulting metals lead, tin, gold, and palladium are sold as commodities. Plastics are grouped by and baled by color and sold to plastics recyclers. Steel is sold to a local metal recycler, and wood from older television cabinets is chipped for use as bio-fuel.

(*Source*: http://www.recycleworks.org/ewaste/ewaste_process.html)

Sequence Words

Look at the underlined words which point to the various steps involved in recycling e-waste. Such words are necessary to show the sequence of steps.

Words which indicate sequence in a discourse are called *sequence words*. Some of the common sequence words are: *firstly, secondly, thirdly, lastly, then, next, afterwards, after, before, subsequently, consequently, later, earlier, thus, finally,* etc. These words have an important function in communication—to indicate the transition from one stage to another.

Learn to use these sequence words effectively in your communication, for they guide your listeners or readers in a friendly way to the purpose of your communication.

Fill in the following table with relevant sequence words and phrases. An example is given below.

	Beginning	**Middle**	**End**
1	To begin with	At this stage	To conclude
2			
3			
4			
5			
6			
7			
8			
9			
10			

Paragraph Writing

Write a paragraph of about 125 words on how e-waste can become a major threat to the Indian environment. Also give a suitable solution to this problem in your paragraph and use sequence words in your paragraph.

Food for Thought

"Waste not, want not," goes the old saying. "Waste not, environment destroy not," is the new one.

UNIT 2

NATURAL RESOURCES

2.1 Water: The Elixir of Life

Thinking and Interaction

Discuss the following questions in pairs and share your answers with the class.

1. Why has elixir always fascinated people?
2. Why is water described as the elixir of life?
3. Why is water known as one of the five basic elements?
4. Why do states fight with each other on account of water?
5. Why do we have to save water for future generations?

Word Power

Match the words in column A with their meaning in column B.

	A	B
1	glacier	a. not normal, distorted
2	depleting	b. a very bad accident causing great damage or loss of life
3	deprived	c. a mass of ice, formed by snow on mountains
4	skewed	d. inability to realise or care how other people feel
5	insensitivity	e. not having the things that are necessary for a pleasant life
6	manicured	f. reducing greatly the quantity or value of something
7	disaster	g. well-cared

Reading

Read the passage below and answer the questions that follow.

We take water so much for granted, but we cannot live without it. Almost three-fourths of the surface of the earth is covered with water. You may ask, so why worry about water?

But have you realised that 97 per cent of the water on earth is in the oceans? This water cannot be directly used to meet any of our daily needs. Almost 2 per cent of the water is stored in ice caps and glaciers and again cannot be used, unless melted. That leaves us with just 1 per cent to meet all the needs of all living beings. This is what we call freshwater, and this is found in ponds, lakes, rivers, and some of this is underground. Can you think of all the uses of water in our daily lives? It is this 1 per cent that meets all these needs.

It is because of this scarcity that we have to be really careful about how this water is used. World over, there is a growing concern about the depleting water sources. The demand for water is the effect of the increased population and industrial growth around the world. In cities like Chennai there is a price on drinking water.

Then there is the reality of the skewed distribution of water. We know that there are some localities in our cities that enjoy water all round the clock, while others are deprived for days. The insensitivity of some is glaring when they use this scarce resource to hose their cars or water their manicured gardens, and all the while, people go thirsty.

There is also the growing pollution of water sources all over the world. This pollution is caused by water released from several industries or sometimes even an accident or disaster in water bodies, which causes the release of pollutants in the water. There are several areas in the country where water has become unfit for drinking because of this.

So next time you keep the tap running, while you brush your teeth or wash your face, think about it. By turning off the tap, you may be helping someone, somewhere, to get a bucketful of water.

Water (from the Old English *waeter*; German *wasser*), in its pure form, is a tasteless and odourless substance that is essential to all known forms of life and is known also as the most universal solvent. It appears colourless to the naked eye in small quantities, though it can be seen to be blue in large quantities or with scientific instruments.

This natural resource is becoming scarcer in certain places, and its availability is a major social and economic concern.

Currently, about one billion people around the world routinely drink unhealthy water. Poor water quality and bad sanitation are killers; some five million deaths a year are <u>due to</u> polluted drinking water.

It is hardly surprising, 90 per cent of all wastewater still goes untreated into local rivers and streams in the developing world. <u>Consequently</u>, some 50 countries, with roughly a third of the world's population, also suffer from medium or high water stress, and 17 of these extract more water annually than is recharged through their natural water cycles. The strain affects surface freshwater bodies like rivers and lakes, and also degrades groundwater resources.

(*Source:* http://www.hindu.com/yw/2006/04/28/stories/2006042800040100.htm)

Comprehension

1. What is freshwater?
2. Why do we have to be careful about water?
3. Why has the demand for water been increasing steadily?
4. What is the problem with the distribution of water?
5. How is water polluted?
6. How do we help others, when we save water?
7. What are the physical and chemical properties of water?
8. What is water stress?

State whether the following are true or false.

1. All available water cannot be used by humans.
2. Demand for water has always been increasing.
3. Some people always face the problem of water scarcity.
4. Industries purify water.
5. All freshwater is potable (drinkable).

Adjective Identification

Identify at least ten adjectives from the passage and list them in the space provided below.

	Adjectives		Adjectives
1		6	
2		7	
3		8	
4		9	
5		10	

Cause and Effect Expressions

Look at the underlined expressions in the passage: *because of, the effect of, causes, caused by, consequently*, and *due to*. They indicate cause and effect relationships. Showing clear cause and effect relationships in writing is one of the hallmarks of good communication.

Look at the example and use the expressions given below in sentences of your own.

owing to
on account of
as a result of
result in
lead to
since
because

1. Water scarcity in Chennai has *lead to* sourcing of water from Veeranam Lake.
2.
3.
4.
5.
6.

Understanding Prepositions

Look at the following words.

about
around
at
by
for
from
in
into
like
of
on
over
round
through
to
with
without

These and many more such words are called prepositions. They usually show relationship between words and indicate time, place, cause, agent, etc. Note that some of them may also be used as a noun, an adjective, a verb, an adverb or a conjunction. For example, look at the sentences given below to see the word 'round' used in different parts of speech.

1. Some people have *round* faces. (adjective)
2. The wheels go *round*. (adverb)
3. The earth moves *round* the sun. (preposition)
4. The final *round* of counting is yet to be completed. (noun)
5. The ship *rounded* the tip of the island. (verb)

Add ten more prepositions to the list and use them in sentences each as two different parts of speech.

Fill in the blanks with suitable prepositions.

The 1500 people of Vellinipatti village near Madurai, who primarily depend .... agriculture .... their livelihood, had to fight .... each other .... every drop .... water available. Over thirty years .... encroachments had turned their 1000-year old, 27-acre water tank .... a ruin and choked water supply. But today, all that has changed. Their tank is overflowing .... water.

Similarly, there are hundreds .... such tanks .... Tamil Nadu, Andhra Pradesh, Karnataka, and Puducherri that have been renovated .... an initiative .... the NGO Dhan Foundation.

Pie Chart

Go back to the second paragraph of the reading passage where availability of water is given in percentages. Represent the same information in the form of a pie chart.

Descriptive Paragraph

Look at the description of water in the seventh paragraph. Describe oxygen in a similar manner.

Food for Thought

"A master of self is not a waster of water."

2.2 The Tree of Life

Thinking and Interaction

Discuss the following questions in pairs and share your answers with the class.

1. What is '*tree of life*'?
2. What are some of the plants and animals that are extinct?
3. Why is biodiversity essential for our planet?
4. Which are some of the major environmental groups in India?

Word Power

Match the words in column A with their meanings in column B.

	A	B
1	extinction	a. incapable of being changed
2	irreversible	b. tending to correct, remedial
3	inglorious	c. a place containing many useful or beautiful things
4	corrective	d. an act of coming to an end, or dying out
5	cornucopia	e. firmly determined
6	trove	f. sections of forest or woods where fires frequently occur
7	finds	g. forming part of a plan to achieve a specific purpose
8	hotspots	h. disgraceful
9	strategic	i. abundant, overflowing supply
10	resolute	j. something found

Listening

Listen to the short talk titled 'Protecting the Tree of Life' and answer the comprehension questions. You may listen to the talk again, if required.

Comprehension

1. Why is extinction a serious environmental problem?
2. What evidence does the author give for extinction?
3. What is 'culture of scientific inquiry'? Would you like to develop such a culture in yourself?
4. Why do we have to protect the environment in strategic terms?
5. What has Edward O. Wilson said about biodiversity conservation?
6. What environmental policy did Indira Gandhi introduce?

State whether the following statements are true or false.

1. Humans have harmed the environment deliberately.

2. Mass consumption is the major cause of environmental degradation.
3. Humans will have great gross natural wealth in the future.
4. Fewer varieties of plants and animals are enough for life on earth.
5. Biodiversity helps in enhancing life.

Tense

Fill in the blanks with suitable tense forms of the verbs given in brackets.

The atmosphere .... (make) life possible on planet Earth because of its three very important functions: it .... (contain) life-giving oxygen, it .... (keep) the earth warm and it .... (absorb) the deadly ultraviolet (UV) rays of the sun's radiation. The earth's atmosphere .... (compose of) numerous gases. The main gases .... (be) nitrogen and oxygen, which .... (make up) 78 per cent and 21 per cent of the volume of air respectively. The remaining one per cent of the atmospheric gases .... (make up) of trace gases, which .... (include) the greenhouse gases—carbon dioxide, methane, nitrous oxide, water vapour, and ozone—so-called because they .... (involve) in the earth's natural greenhouse effect which .... (keep) the planet warmer than it .... (be) without an atmosphere. The trace gas ozone .... (be) important in protecting life on earth. Ozone .... (be) a colourless and odourless gas. It .... (perform) an important function of filtering out the harmful UV rays from the sun's radiation.

Pie Chart

In the listening passage, atmospheric gases are given in percentage. Convert the same information into a pie chart.

Food for Thought

"Both life and knowledge can be derived from trees."

2.3 Land Use Plan: Interview with Dr George B. Schaller

Thinking and Interaction

Discuss the following questions in pairs and share your answers with the class.

1. Which scientists study plants and animals?
2. What is the WWF? What does it do?
3. Which famous author is closely associated with the Indian tiger?
4. Which Indian political leader is well known for championing the cause of the environment?
5. Why do we have to protect the environment at all?

Word Power

Match the words in column A with their meaning in column B.

	A	B
1	conservation	a. able to continue over a period of time
2	project	b. catching and killing animals without permission
3	heritage	c. sad and hopeless
4	critical	d. an animal that is hunted and killed for food by another animal
5	tremendous	e. to suffer the sudden inability to continue or work correctly
6	dismal	f. of the greatest importance to the way things might happen
7	sustainable	g. a planned activity
8	prey	h. very great in amount or level, extremely good
9	poaching	i. the prevention of loss, waste, damage and destruction
10	collapse	j. things that have been passed on from earlier generations

Reading

Read the interview given below and answer the questions that follow.

[Dr George B. Schaller is a pioneer in field biology. He says it is possible to achieve economic growth without destroying the environment and losing wildlife. With his meticulous research four decades ago and the resulting scientific treatise on India's wildlife titled "The Deer and the Tiger", Dr Schaller

significantly influenced India's first major conservation policies. As Vice-President of the New York-based Wildlife Conservation Society, he now steers its international conservation programs, covering wild species that range from rare sheep in the Pamir Mountains to tigers in tropical forests and cheetahs in the Iranian desert. He answers some of the questions of G. Ananthakrishnan.]

G. A.: What is India's conservation record since your path-breaking work?

G. S.: I made a very small first step, and described what I actually saw in the forest. Since then the best tiger biologists like Ullas Karanth have put tiger studies on a firm basis. How to census them, how to monitor them. . . Raghu Chundawat and a whole lot of others are adding to the knowledge. Now you have a really solid background so you know what must be done and what government policy there should be and how local people can be involved. That's how it is normally. You start science with small questions and other people continue and it spreads out. It is satisfying to see Indian knowledge and so many good biologists. The Wildlife Conservation Society (WCS) has been funding projects here for years. We have two projects in Ladakh and one in Arunachal. WCS has set up a very good model for tigers in South India. So when tigers are in trouble in other places, you can see in Bandipur and Mudumalai that they are not heavily poached.

G. A.: Is there hope that we can save much of what is left of natural spaces, given the pressure for economic growth?

G. S.: You can have development, but it has to be done carefully. The government has to have its policies. It has to decide that this area we are going to save, we are going to guard it, and work with local communities. But governments tend to want to make money right now. Politicians don't think of the future almost by definition, and so there is very little long term planning. A country like India, or for that matter any country, must have a land use plan. Certain areas should be designated as part of the natural heritage. Countries are at a critical point. Consumption is increasing far faster than population. They cannot afford that. They need leaders. Indira Gandhi did a tremendous service by raising awareness on environment and wildlife. The U.S. had Teddy Roosevelt a hundred years ago.

G. A.: China and India experience severe pressure on the environment. We have lost a lot.

G. S.: You have lost a lot, but you still have a lot. You still have quite a bit of forest. You still have tigers and leopards. But the problem has been in the last few years, the government has been quite lax. They sat back and said, okay, things are pretty good. Meanwhile, how many thousands of leopards have been killed just to send skins to Tibet? There needs to be much more detailed monitoring.

In China, the outlook is open for most species. For tigers it is questionable and it is on a downhill slide, almost at the bottom, but for most species and habitats, they can do it. The Chinese government has been extremely supportive. When I started work there in 1980 there were about a dozen reserves, now they have about 2,000, totalling about 15 per cent of the country.

G. A.: Talking about development, many view this as an economic versus environment question...

G. S.: That is a far too simpleminded way to look at it. What you need to measure among other things is the services that the natural environment provides. Cleaning the air, cleaning the water, the genetic background to rehabilitate areas . . . you can in rough ways actually measure it. The billions of rupees the forest provides for free that would cost you otherwise.

G. A.: You have suggested the creation of a wildlife sanctuary there.

G. S.: Yes. This includes Pakistan, Afghanistan, China, and Tajikistan, and I have been working in all those countries making censuses. I find that the Marco Polo sheep move across international borders. But these are animals that attract attention. Trophy hunters like to shoot it and everybody knows about it. Therefore, it is a good symbol on which conservation can be based. I am trying to get the four countries together to make a land use plan for that part of the Pamirs.

In China, I am doing something similar in the Tibetan plateau. You have the Chiru, the Tibetan antelope that has the finest wool and India is involved in the trade—the Shahtoosh business. The NGOs have been working very hard to reduce it, but the wool still comes from Tibet. China has worked hard to control poaching, and it is down a lot, but it still continues.

G. A.: What is the state of the tiger?

G. S.: The only country where the tiger population has increased recently is Russia. The Wildlife Conservation Society and others had an intensive programme there. They have tried to increase prey numbers by reducing poaching. That looks hopeful. Whereas next door in China, it is in absolutely dismal condition. The Siberian tiger from Northeastern Russia is the occasional visitor and as far as anybody knows there are no residents. We don't know of any breeding populations left in China, just some scattered individuals. But in countries like Cambodia, Thailand, Myanmar, yes, most definitely they can increase with protection and monitoring. Ullas Karanth has set up the Tigers Forever programme of the WCS in some areas. In Laos, in most places the tigers are gone, but there are patches where they can be maintained and definitely increased. Nepal has been doing all right, except now there is political turmoil and poaching. Sumatra still has a few large reserves.

G. A.: What would you say to someone who said extinction is nothing new and that it happened in the past?

G. S.: That statement is perfectly true. But the problem is it has been calculated that extinction rates are a 100 to a 1,000 times greater than they were in the past. In other words it is so fast that things don't have much time to adapt. We are dealing with tens of thousands of species. Most of the insects, the soil nematodes and so on . . . what is their function? How many of those species can you lose before the whole thing collapses? When you don't understand something, the best thing to do is to save all the pieces so that you have an option in the future.

G. A.: Edward Wilson (the naturalist) said that the earth's sustainable capacity was exceeded by population demands in 1978. . .

G. S.: That certainly sounds reasonable considering the consumption. The population curve may well level off in the middle of this century but the consumption curve will keep going up because you have well over two billion people in India and China alone who want to consume more.

Look at the cell phone. The phone has a little mineral in it called coltan. It is a capacitor that intensifies the energy that enables this little machine to send signals. Coltan is mainly mined in the eastern Congo, by thousands of people living and digging in the forest. They need meat. Therefore, they eat gorillas and elephants. So your little cell phone helps kill gorillas. Then you had a cup of tea this morning. Somewhere rainforest is falling to plant more tea.

(*Source:* http://www.hindu.com/2006/09/23/stories/2006092305741100.htm)

Comprehension

1. What does Schaller mean by "land use plan'?
2. How can political leaders help in protecting the environment?
3. What is the basic conflict between economic development and environmental destruction?
4. Why does Schaller talk about the cell phone?
5. What is the connection between a cup of tea and the rainforest?

State whether the following are true or false.

1. Local people have an important role to play in tiger conservation projects.
2. Politicians plan well for the protection of nature.
3. China has made considerable progress in tiger conservation.
4. Those who know about trophy hunting take steps to save the Marco Polo sheep.

5. Tigers in Russia have a safer place for living than tigers in China.
6. Humans do not truly understand the function of animals and insects in the order of nature.
7. Consumption curve level will become normal in course of time.

Note-taking

Fill in the blanks with relevant names from the passage.

An example is given for you. You do not have to show relationships between the categories.

Conservationists	Political leaders	Countries	Animals
Edward Wilson		The US	Marco Polo sheep

Word Power

In the space provided below give antonyms for the following words from the text.

	A	B
1	uphill	
2	production	
3	hostile	
4	destruction	
5	bright	

Verbs and Verb-making Suffixes

Classify the following words, taken from the text, into five different word groups and fill in the table. Write the name of each category in the top column.

made
described
put
to census
to monitor
adding
involved
have
continue
spreads
satisfying
funding
set up
are
can
see
poached
going
to guard
think
tend
to want
to make
designated
increasing

If you have any doubt about the group to which these words belong, check the context in which these words are used.

1.	2.	3.	4.	5.

Look at the following table with examples of verbs made using suffixes. Give your own examples in the last column.

	Suffix	Examples	Your examples
1	-ise	emphasise, energise	
2	-ate	appreciate, generate	
3	-fy	satisfy, intensify	
4	-en	fasten, deepen, strengthen	
5	-e	breathe	

Dialogue Writing and Role Play

G. Ananthakrishnan's interview with Dr George B. Schaller helps us understand the importance of the land use plan. Assume that you represent an environmental activist group and have the responsibility of persuading the minister for environment of your state to preserve the land. You get an appointment to meet him. Write out the dialogue between you and the minister. Later, two students may play these roles for the entire class.

Product Description

Look at Schaller's description of the cell phone. Choose any two products which are used in our daily life and describe them with a focus on how they affect our environment.

Food for Thought

"Land or sand, nature has the upper hand."

2.4 Painted Storks

Thinking and Interaction

Discuss the following questions in pairs and share your answers with the class.

1. Why do birds and animals move from one place to another, especially during winter?
2. How do they trace the route back to their original habitats?
3. What are the electronic gadgets used for tracking the movement of people and goods?

Word Power

Match the words in column A with their meanings in column B.

	A	B
1	cruising	a. the science which studies the movement of gases and the way solid bodies like aircraft move through them
2	charter	b. travelling on ships for pleasure
3	traverse	c. becoming smaller in size or amount
4	celestial	d. in or from the air
5	innate	e. negotiate
6	nondescript	f. wandering
7	aerial	g. very ordinary
8	migratory	h. of or from the sky
9	aerodynamics	i. a quality one is born with
10	dwindling	j. to travel through an area

Reading

Read the passage and answer the questions that follow.

Even after cruising beneath the Pacific and Atlantic oceans for years, commanders of the state-of-the-art US-made SSBN Typhoon-class nuclear submarine refer to the satellite-fed global positioning system and electronic gadgets to assess their position and charter their course back to the bases. But what mechanism do pelicans and painted storks follow to traverse the 12,000 km from the snow deserts of Siberia to the coastal village of Telineelapuram in Srikakulam district of Andhra Pradesh?

Every year, over 3,000 pelicans and painted storks make their way from Siberia to this nondescript village during September and stay on till March-end.

"They simply go by celestial navigation. Some researchers say the birds possess innate sensory objects in their brain that can trace the waves generated by the Earth's magnetic field," B. Bharatha Lakshmi, Professor of Zoology, Andhra University, said.

Researchers at Andhra University said the birds had been following this aerial route for the past 15 years. The migratory movement was first noticed over 15 years ago. At that time, the number of birds exceeded 10,000. Today, the figure has dwindled to about 3,000. Apart from avoiding the harsh Siberian winter and food scarcity, the birds come here for breeding as well.

Flying in 'V' shaped groups, the older birds lead the way. Professor Lakshmi said scientists worldwide have pointed out that the 'V' formation scientifically creates a vacuum in the middle to facilitate the younger ones to use less energy. "Many aircraft manufacturers follow the aerodynamics and flying patterns of these migratory birds in their research and development programmes. The birds fly at an average speed of 90 kmph and can do over 800 km at a stretch," she said.

Both the pelicans and the painted storks are sensitive to pollution. Professor Lakshmi attributed the dwindling number of the birds to a fire accident at Telineelapuram a few years ago and to increased tree felling. "Poaching is rare but it does happen at the feeding ground," she added.

(*Source:* http://www.hindu.com/2006/04/10/stories/2006041001702000.htm)

Comprehension

1. What are the devices used by submariners to go back to their bases?
2. What mechanisms do migratory birds use to get back to their homes?
3. Why does the author compare submarines with birds?
4. How long have the birds been following the route?
5. Why do the Siberian birds come to Andhra Pradesh?
6. What is special about the flight formation of birds?
7. Why do manufacturers follow the flying pattern of birds for making their aircrafts?
8. Why has the number of pelicans and painted storks visiting Andhra Pradesh reduced?

Understanding Nouns

Look at the nouns listed below and their endings. Give two more examples of nouns formed using each of the suffixes. An example is given for you.

Noun	Suffix	Noun 1	Noun 2
commander	-er	researcher	manufacturer
village	-age		
navigation	-ion		
electricity	-ity		
movement	-ment		
poaching	-ing		

Process and Person Nouns

Nouns may refer to a process or a person. For example, *experimentation* and *experimenter* are both nouns, one referring to the process of experimentation and another to the person who conducts the experiment.

Fill in the blanks with suitable forms of the words. An example is given for you. The first noun refers to a process and the second noun refers to a person.

	verb	noun (process)	noun (person)
1	navigate	navigation	navigator
2	migrate		
3	paint		
4	facilitate		
5	poach		
6	manufacture		
7	protect		
8	conserve		
9	organise		
10	visualise		

Paragraph Writing

Write a paragraph of about 125 words on the protection of migratory birds that come to India.

Food for Thought

"Even if human beings don't learn, nature continues to teach."

2.5 Platinum

Thinking and Interaction

Discuss the following questions in pairs and share your answers with the class.

1. What are the commonly used metals for making jewellery?
2. What are white metals?
3. Which metal are rich people more interested in now?

Word Power

Match the words in column A to their meanings in column B.

	A	B
1	precious	a. causing less or no allergic sensation
2	hypoallergenic	b. keeping elsewhere
3	coveted	c. a device on a car that reduces the amount of poisonous gas that is released from the exhaust
4	exquisite	d. material made of a network of wire or thread
5	scratches	e. a small device which is put inside someone's chest in order to help the heart beat at the correct speed
6	displacement	f. very beautiful, delicate
7	pliability	g. of great value because of being rare
8	mesh	h. desired strongly, especially something that belongs to someone else
9	catalytic converter	i. cuts or damages on a surface
10	pacemaker	j. able to bend easily without breaking or cracking

Reading

Read the passage and answer the questions that follow.

Platinum is pure, rare, eternal, and versatile; it is a precious and special metal. It is pure, an expression of integrity, and a reflection of inner truth. Its purity endows it with a brilliant white lustre. This helps to reflect the true radiance of diamonds. Because it is generally 95% pure (18 karat gold is 75% pure), platinum jewellery does not fade or tarnish and keeps its looks for a lifetime. Platinum's purity makes it hypoallergenic and ideal for those with sensitive skin.

It is rare, the coveted treasure of discerning individuals. There is very little platinum on this earth and it is found in very few places around the world. This exquisite metal is thirty times rarer than gold. In fact, it is estimated that if all the platinum in the world were poured into one Olympic swimming pool, it would be scarcely deep enough to cover your ankles. Gold would fill more than three pools. Platinum's rarity makes it exclusive and distinctive—a celebration of your individuality

Platinum jewellery is the perfect choice for a lifetime of everyday wear. Its density and weight make it more durable than other jewellery metals. It does not wear away and holds precious stones firmly and securely. Like all precious metals, platinum scratches. However, the scratch on a platinum piece is merely a displacement of the metal and none of its volume is lost. So, even though wearing it each and every day may leave an impression on the surface, it remains what it was—a symbol for all things eternal.

In addition to its strength and density, platinum has another remarkable quality—pliability. It is so pliable, that just one gram of the metal can be drawn to produce a fine wire over one mile (almost 2 km) long. This quality has enabled jewellers to create some amazing versatile platinum mesh accessories, which could not be fashioned from other precious metals. It is also in demand in other fields—it is used in industry, most notably in catalytic converters. It also plays an important role in medicine. It is not affected by the oxidising reaction of blood, has excellent conductivity, and is compatible with living tissue. Because of these properties, platinum is used for pacemakers. At present, more than 50,000 people are living healthily on pacemakers. Platinum is a life-saving metal for these people.

(*Source:* http://www.preciousplatinum.com/output/Page26.asp)

Comprehension

1. What are the special qualities of platinum?
2. What are the uses of platinum?
3. How is platinum 'a celebration of your individuality'?
4. What is the purpose of the author in writing this text?
5. Who do you think is the target audience of this passage?

Understanding Adjectives

Look at the adjectives used to describe platinum in the first paragraph.

pure
rare
eternal
versatile
precious
special

Underline the other adjectives used in the passage.

Using the table below, classify the various adjectives into different groups according to their form in different degrees of comparison. For example, pure has three forms: pure, purer, and purest.

	Positive	Comparative	Superlative
1	pure	purer	purest
2			
3			
4			
5			
6			

(Contd...)

7			
8			
9			
10			

Degrees of Comparison

Look at the following sentence.

This exquisite metal is thirty times *rarer* than gold.

The rarity of platinum is compared with gold and is given in comparative degree. Such comparisons can be made for two things. Look at another example.

Blood is *thicker* than water.

Write comparative statements for the following.

1. lakes and rivers
2. radio and TV
3. table fan and ceiling fan
4. bicycle and motor cycle
5. silver and gold

Double Adjectives

There are some nouns from which more than one adjective can be derived. For instance, '*impressive*' and '*impressionable*' are adjectives derived from the noun, '*impression*' but they have different meanings. Similarly, '*industrious*' and '*industrial*' are derived from '*industry*'.

Look up the dictionary to check the meanings of the following pairs of adjectives and use them in sentences of your own.

	noun	**adjective 1**	**adjective 2**
1	illustration	illustrative	illustrious
2	education	educative	educational
3	creation	creative	creational
4	sense	sensitive	sensible
5	response	responsive	responsible
6	continuation	continuous	continual
7	consideration	considerate	considerable
8	society	social	sociable
9	description	descriptive	describable
10	consumption	consumptive	consumable

Paragraph Writing

1. *Write a paragraph of about 125 words comparing platinum with gold.*
2. *Write a paragraph of about 125 words on the industrial uses of platinum.*
3. *Compare the two paragraphs and note the differences. Your purpose in writing decides the nature of the paragraph.*

Food for Thought

"Jubilees are measured in precious metals."

Flowchart

Read the following passage and draw a flow chart to represent the process of extracting platinum.

Platinum mining and production entail extreme difficulties. Extraction, concentration and refining of the metal require quite complex processes that may take up to six months. It is estimated that in order to produce a single ounce of platinum a volume of 7 to 12 tons of ore must be processed.

Extraction

Usually platinum mining is underground although there is some open-pit mining. The extraction stage of platinum is labour-intensive. Miners bore holes with hand-held pneumatic drills and blast them with explosives. Afterward ore is removed and transported to the surface. Normally, mill-head grades of BIC (the measure for the PGM content for the ore) are between 4 and 7 grams per ton.

Once in the surface, ore is crushed and milled in order to obtain smaller rock particles and to expose the minerals which contain the PGM. In a "froth flotation" process these particles are mixed with water and special reagents, before air is pumped through the liquid. As a result bubbles to which the PGM-containing particles adhere are created and they float to the surface. This flotation concentrate is removed as a soapy froth. The PGM content, at this stage, varies between 100 and 1000 grams per ton. In order to obtain the maximum amount of PGM, the material, which fails to float, goes through a second milling and flotation process.

Concentration

The flotation concentrate, once dried, is smelted in an electric furnace at temperatures that may be over 1500°C. Then, a matter which contains the valuable metals is separated from the unwanted minerals that are discarded. After being periodically tapped, air is blown through this matte in the converters with the purpose of removing iron and sulfur. Now the "converter matte" PGM content is higher than 1400 grams per ton.

Refining

At a base metal refinery, nickel, copper and cobalt are separated from the PGM using standard electrolytic techniques. Residues in which PGM are concentrated are obtained. The last stage of the platinum production requires the separation and purification of the platinum group metals, apart from gold and small amounts of silver. This is the most difficult and intricate part of the process, combining solvent extraction, distillation and ion-exchange techniques. Finally, the soluble metals, which dissolve in hydrochloric acid and chlorine gas, are obtained: first gold and then palladium and platinum. The insoluble PGM are the last to be extracted, platinum.

(*Source:* http://www.unctad.org/infocomm/anglais/platinum/chain.htm)

Understanding Vocabulary

In the first and second units, you learnt about the way in which prefixes and suffixes are used to form words—adverbs, nouns, adjectives and verbs. If you understand that one word has several forms and functions, you will be able to improve and strengthen your vocabulary tremendously. Given below is a table of verbs, nouns, adjectives, and adverbs to show how forms of a word are derived.

Word Forms

	Verb	Noun	Adjective	Adverb
1	attract	attraction	attractive	attractively
2	communicate	communication	communicative	communicatively
3	relate	relation	relative	relatively
4	specify	specification	specific	specifically
5	interact	interaction	interactive	interactively
6	normalise	normalisation	normal	normally
7	activate	activity	active	actively
8	tolerate	tolerance	tolerable	tolerably
9	accept	acceptance	acceptable	acceptably
10	prefer	preference	preferential	preferentially
11	originate	origin	original	originally
12	educate	education	educational	educationally
13	describe	description	descriptive	descriptively
14	express	expression	expressive	expressively
15	generate	generation	generative	generatively
16	structure	structure	structural	structurally
17	provide	provision	provisional	provisionally
18	continue	continuation	continuous	continuously
19	attend	attention	attentive	attentively
20	visualise	visualisation	visual	visually
21	recognise	recognition	recognisable	recognisably
22	create	creation	creative	creatively
23	innovate	innovation	innovative	innovatively
24	present	presentation	presentable	presentably
25	emote	emotion	emotional	emotionally
26	equivocate	equivocation	equivocal	equivocally
27	persuade	persuasion	persuasive	persuasively
28	produce	production	productive	productively
29	add	addition	additional	additionally
30	react	reaction	reactive	reactively

Food for Thought

"Word power is world power."

UNIT 3

INFRASTRUCTURE DEVELOPMENT

3.1 Power Supply

Thinking and Interaction

Discuss the following questions in pairs and share your answers with the class.

1. What are the different meanings of power?
2. What does power mean in the term 'power supply'?
3. Why do we in India have a shortfall in power supply?
4. How do individuals and organisations cope with erratic and inadequate power supply?
5. How is power important for the development of our country?

Discuss with your partner and complete the table with relevant details of two conventional sources of power.

	Features	**Hydro power**	**Thermal power**
1	source		
2	place of production		
3	cost of production		
4	reliability and dependability		
5	impact on the environment		

(Contd...)

6	impact on the economy		
7.	safety of employees and users		

Word Power

Match the words in column A to their meanings in column B.

	A	B
1	trotting out	a. increasing the size or value
2	gigawatts	b. giving opinions which have already been stated
3	augmentation	c. stunning, powerful blow
4	whammy	d. one thousand million watts

Reading

Read the passage and answer the questions that follow.

While Union Power Minister Sushil Kumar Shinde is trotting out a host of reasons why the 10th Plan power generation capacity is less than 50 per cent of the target, China has announced that it is slowing down the expansion of power utilities because generating capacities have come up too fast.

A Bloomberg report from Beijing says China, which has plans to up expansion by 15 percent in 2007, will press the brakes on the 2008 expansion program because of concerns of possible excess supply in the market in the world's fastest growing economy. "Power capacity growth will slow down in 2008", Sun Yaowei, a Deputy Director at the State Regulatory Commission, has said in Beijing. China may add less than 70 gigawatts of capacity next year, compared with this year's projection of as much as 95 gigawatts, he said.

Those are figures that would leave India gasping. Power generation capacity addition during the 10th Plan period (2002–07) is expected to be just 31,000 MW—way below the scaled down target of 41,000 MW. The performance was no better in the 9th Plan, when capacity augmentation was about 60 per cent below target. In short, India has added less capacity in 10 years than China has done in one year. That is a powerful whammy indeed.

China, on the other hand, will be able to balance its power demand and supply after four years of shortages. This, when its consumption increased by 13.5 per cent to 2,834.4 million megawatt hours last year, and utilisation hours of power plants dropped by 3.7 per cent due to expanded capacity.

(*Source*: *Business World*, Vol. 26, No. 47, 16.4.2007, p. 14)

Comprehension

1. What does S. K. Shinde say about the 10th plan power generation capacity?
2. What does Sun Yaowei say about the Chinese power generation capacity?
3. Why did India reduce its target capacity of power generation in the 10th plan period?
4. What has China done in one year in the power sector?
5. How long did China have power shortages?

Complete the table with relevant information from the passage.

	Features	India	China
1	power production capacity		
2	production plans		
3	projected target		
4	actual achievement		
5	supply and demand		
6	addition of capacity		
7	duration of achievement		
8	percentage of consumption		

Paragraph Writing

Use the notes you have taken in the table and write a paragraph of about 125 words on the comparative strengths and weaknesses of India and China in the power sector.

Comparative Expressions

Look at the following comparative expressions.

while
less than
compared with
no better than
on the other hand

These expressions are used to compare two ideas, things, or persons. Learn to use them in sentences of your own.

List five more comparative expressions.

1.
2.
3.
4.
5.

The following passage compares soap with detergent. Fill in the blanks with suitable comparative expressions.

Soaps are sodium or potassium salts of long chain carboxylic acids (fatty acids) .... detergents are salts of long chain sulphates or sulphonates. Hence, soaps and detergents have a long organic tail with a (negatively charged) polar head, that is, they are anionic in nature. The organic tail is hydrophobic (water-hating) but lyophilic (oil-loving) .... the polar head is hydrophilic (water-loving) and lyophobic (oil-hating).

The cleansing action of both detergents and soaps is about the same. Dirty clothes and skin have oily layers. Simple wetting and rinsing of such clothes and skin would not remove the dirt because the oil is immiscible in water. .... a detergent or soap is used along with water, the lyophilic tails of the detergent species tag on to the oily layer and the hydrophilic heads face the water. The agitation causes the oily matter to break into small droplets and is trapped inside the lyophilic 'cage' formed by the detergent molecules.

Thus the oily matter is kept suspended in water. The structure formed by the detergent molecules where the oil is trapped is called a micelle. The role of the detergent molecules is to prevent the oil droplets from coalescing once again and returning to the cloth.

The differences between soaps and detergents stem from their sensitivities to hard water and acidic conditions. .... hard water (which contains magnesium and calcium ions in .... permitted levels) is used, the soap precipitates out as calcium or magnesium salts.

................, the detergents are .... prone to complexation with the metal ion and hence would be .... affected by the hard water. Likewise, the soap would precipitate out under acid conditions as the carboxylic acid group would be protonated, ... the detergent would survive acidic conditions better.

(*Source*: http://www.hindu.com/seta/2006/04/13/stories/2006041302191700.htm)

Sentence Structure

Read the text on power supply again. The sentences may look long and appear to have a number of sentence parts. Hence, they may seem complex and difficult for some readers to understand. But, if you understand the basic sentence structures and the varying combinations of the elements that make sentences, you will be able to interpret any kind of sentence easily.

There are five basic sentence patterns and these are determined by the way in which sentence elements combine together. These elements are: subject, verb, object, complement and adjunct.

Adjunct is an additional element, not essential for making sense of a sentence. It may come at the beginning, middle, or, at the end of a sentence. Look at the following example: Power cuts are common *in all areas*. The phrase *in all areas* gives some extra information about power cuts. Without the prepositional phrase, the sentence would read as follows: *Power cuts are common*. This sentence would still make sense.

Given below are the five basic sentence structures.

1. Subject + Verb
   Example: Power generation has slowed down.
2. Subject + Verb+ Complement
   Example: Power is insufficient.
3. Subject + Verb + Object
   Example: China can sell power.

4. Subject + Verb + Object + Object
   Example: Tamil Nadu gives farmers free power.
5. Subject + Verb + Object + Complement
   Example: The UN declared 2005 the International Year of Physics.

Identify the basic structures in the following sentences.

1. India imports oil.
2. BCCI named Dravid captain for the England tour.
3. The Buddha smiles.
4. Air pollution causes asthma.
5. We sent the refugees food and clothes.

Write a sentence of your own for each of the basic structures.

Group Discussion

In groups of four or five, discuss how India can increase its power production capacity and meet energy needs comfortably without affecting the environment. The group leaders may then report their views to the class.

3.2 Industrial Park

Thinking and Interaction

Discuss the following questions in pairs and share your answers with the class.

1. What is a park?
2. What are the different kinds of parks you are familiar with?
3. What is an industrial park?
4. Give some examples of industrial parks from your state.
5. What is an SEZ?
6. Why do farmers and some political parties oppose SEZs?

Word Power

Match the words in column A to their meanings in column B.

	A	B
1	zoning	a. facilities for the public
2	delimited	b. regular journeys between home and work
3	utilities	c. a prosperous residential area outside the suburbs of a town
4	glut	d. the act of deciding what particular use an area should have
5	cult	e. an area of land in a town that was previously used for industry and where new buildings can be built
6	exurbs	f. boundaries fixed
7	commutes	g. something that has become very popular with a group of people
8	brownfield	h. excess

Listening

Listen to a short lecture titled 'Industrial Park' and answer the questions given below.

Comprehension

1. What is an industrial park?
2. Where are industrial parks located?
3. What are the two kinds of industrial parks?
4. What are the objectives of setting up of industrial parks?
5. What is the significance of 'no special environmental safeguards'?
6. What was the trend in the US from the 1970s to the 1990s?
7. Why does David Brooks say that contact between urban and suburban people is lost?
8. What are the criticisms against industrial parks?

Look at the following table and notice the differences in British English and American English.

	British English	American English
1	industrial estate	industrial park
2	flat	apartment
3	lift	elevator
4	railway	railroad
5	mobile phone	cell phone

Complete the table given below with examples of words in British English and their American English equivalents.

	British	American		British	American
1			11		
2			12		
3			13		
4			14		
5			15		
6			16		
7			17		
8			18		
9			19		
10			20		

Give the American equivalent of the following British English words.

1. lorry –
2. financial –
3. tap –
4. pavement –
5. autumn –

Give the British English equivalent of the following American English words.

1. gas –
2. engineer –
3. first floor –
4. mail –
5. movie –

Dialogue Writing and Role Play

Form groups of four or five. Imagine that a British and an American are having a conversation with each other and that they are having trouble understanding each other. Assume that they understand each other words differently and so are unable to carry on the conversation. Resolve the misunderstanding by introducing an Indian who understands both British and American English. Write out the dialogue as a group activity. Later, the teacher may ask the group that has produced the best script to enact the same in the class.

Insight

British English and American English differ not only in vocabulary but also in pronunciation and grammar. Learn these differences for effective international and intercultural communication. It is useful to be aware of other varieties of English like Canadian English, Australian English, and, of course, Indian English.

3.3 Highway to Danger

Thinking and Interaction

Discuss the following questions in pairs and share your answers with the class.

1. What are the highways you are familiar with?
2. Why do accidents occur frequently on highways?
3. How can we prevent such accidents?
4. What measures does the government take to improve the highways?

Word Power

Match the words in column A to their meanings in column B.

	A	B
1	impunity	a. walking across a road at a place where it is not allowed
2	impose	b. the act of looking for trouble or danger in an area
3	jurisdiction	c. officially force a rule, tax, punishment, etc.
4	maim	d. freedom from punishment
5	fatal	e. impossible to repair or make it right again
6	restrictive	f. the authority of an official organisation to make legal decisions
7	mishaps	g. to injure a person severely
8	irreparable	h. causing death
9	jaywalking	i. unlucky accidents
10	patrol	j. limiting the freedom of someone or preventing someone from growing

Read the questions and the paragraphs that follow and match the questions with the paragraphs that have the answers to them.

a. Which highways offer a pleasant drive?

b. Why is driving within the city so tiresome?
c. What are the causes of road safety problems?
d. Why was a spot estimate of traffic density undertaken?
e. What is the finding of the spot estimate?
f. How many people use the roads everyday?
g. How many fatal accidents have occurred?
h. What does the number of accidents signify?

1. --.

Long-distance driving is fun, but not within the city. The dense traffic and frequent automatic signals on all major roads make driving more a pain than pleasure. Add to it the mindless driving one comes across—violating one-ways, crashing through the red light about five seconds before it turns green, cyclists and two-wheelers weaving between motorised vehicles to creep up as close to the middle of a junction far away from the stop line, vehicles crossing the stop line with impunity, and if you happen to believe in stop lines, you would not be spared by those more enthusiastic in the margin of advantage beyond the line—and you have the spices for a chaos-curry. Everything that a long-distance driving enthusiast hates. But once you are beyond the city limits and hit the highway, you feel like a free bird ready to take off. And you do.

2. --.

The sudden sense of freedom may impose a high cost on other users of the free(dom)way. Not all highways—the East Coast Road, Old Mamallapuram Road, the Grand South Trunk Road, Poonamallee High Road, and the Grand North Trunk Road—have a solid median keeping the two-way traffic apart. The distance between the two entities should be as large as possible and there should be shrubs and trees in the separating stretch so that the glare of high beams at night does not have a dangerous blinding effect.

3. --.

The total length of highways within Greater Chennai (that is outside the city limits but within the region defined as Greater Chennai which still falls under the jurisdiction of the Joint Police Commissioner-Traffic) is 184 km. As the Highways Department did not give an estimate of the traffic density along the major highways beyond the city limits but within Greater Chennai, a spot estimate was done at three points beyond the city—Grand North Trunk near Red Hills lake, East Coast Road near Fisherman's Cove, and the National Highway near Vandalur zoo.

4. --.

The average peak hour traffic density per minute at these points was 22, off-peak hours it was 16 and after 9 p.m. it was 27 at the three spots. It would not be deemed an error to say that the average per minute traffic density is 20. That means 1,200 vehicles zip at high speeds along these highways every hour and an amazing 28,800 vehicles roar up and down these roads everyday. A slight error by anyone will lead to crash that could kill some, and maim some more.

5. --.

"There were 348 fatal accidents between January 1 and August 7, 2006 compared to 438 up to August 7, 2005 and the total number of accidents up to the same date this year has been 3,090 compared to 3,751 for both Chennai City and Greater Chennai," said Sunil Kumar, Joint Commissioner of Police (Traffic).

6. --.

If you assume that there are at least two persons on an average on every vehicle (which is not a restrictive assumption, given that truck drivers have at least two persons in the cabin, buses carry at least 60 people, while two-wheelers tend to have a pillion rider) there are 57,600 people shooting down these highways every 24 hours. As there are 184 km of highways within Greater Chennai, 1,05,98,400 roaduser-kilometres are being covered everyday.

7. --.

Accidents always happen at a point of time and space. Given the fatalities, it works out to 0.00328 per cent of the total roaduser-kilometres everyday along these stretches of highways. A small number really, but a massive loss if you think of the lifetime earning potential of those who died in these mishaps. If you add the irreparable loss of a dear one to the family, the loss cannot be quantified in rupees, dollars or euros.

8. --.

"Jaywalking and senseless driving are the main causes," said Sunil Kumar. What about poor policing and the absence of an active highway patrol being a contributing cause? The traffic officers find that hard to accept, but all contributing causes need to be identified and eliminated one by one. That alone will make our roads safer, and will show that even policy makers realise how valuable human life is.

(*Source*: http://www.hinduonnet.com/thehindu/mp/2006/08/29/stories/2006082900040400.htm)

Comprehension

State whether the following are true or false.

1. A long distance driving enthusiast does not like the city roads because these roads are not maintained well.
2. The East Coast Road is a freeway.
3. It is not the responsibility of the Highways Department to give an estimate of the traffic density.
4. The number of accidents have come down recently.
5. The volume of traffic on the highways is very huge.
6. The number of accidents is not so significant as the loss of valuable individual lives.
7. Careless motorists alone are responsible for most of the accidents.

Complete the following sentences.

1. The reasons for the chaos on city roads are ....
2. The shrubs and trees on the median are meant to ....
3. Greater Chennai covers the areas of ....
4. The study reveals that .... ply at high speeds every hour.
5. 1,05,98,400 road-user kilometers are calculated for ....
6. The major causes of accidents on the highways are ....

Homograph

A homograph is a word which is spelled like another but pronounced differently and has a different meaning. For example, '*minute*' as noun means each of the sixty equal parts of an hour and '*minute*' as adjective means careful and accurate. Another example is '*bow*' which is used both as a noun and a verb.

Use each of the words listed below in two sentences in the forms given in brackets.

1. converse (noun and verb)
2. console (noun and verb)
3. wind (noun and verb)
4. perfect (adjective and verb)
5. refuse (noun and verb)

Can you list a few more homographs?

1.
2.

3.
4.
5.

Homophone

A homophone is a word that is pronounced like another word but has a different spelling and different meaning. For example, the words '*not*' and '*knot*' are pronounced alike but have different meanings. '*Not*' is a word that is used to form negatives and '*knot*' means a joint made by tying together two pieces or ends of string, rope, etc.

Use each of the following sets of words in sentences.

1. pray and prey
2. brake and break
3. rain, reign, and rein
4. strait and straight
5. write and right

Can you list at least five more pairs of homophones?

1.
2.
3.
4.
5.

Listed below are some words commonly confused for one another. Use these words in sentences of your own to bring out their meanings clearly.

1. patrol and petrol
2. maim and mime
3. affect and effect
4. accept and except
5. pore and pour
6. stationary and stationery
7. discreet and discrete
8. complement and compliment
9. canvass and canvas
10. counsel and council

Role Play

Imagine that the Joint Commissioner of Police (Traffic) has arranged for a meeting to discuss the various problems of road safety with a view to finding some practicable solutions. The participants are:

1. *The Chief Engineer, National Highways Authority of India*
2. *The Chief Engineer, State Highways Department*
3. *The Secretary, Transport Department*
4. *The Commissioner, City Corporation*
5. *The President, Road Safety Association, an NGO*

Five students may play these roles. Each one should be able to point out a particular problem and offer a solution to the same after which all participants may discuss the merits of the solutions offered.

Understanding Letter to the Editor

Every newspaper has a regular 'letter to the editor' column where readers voice their opinions on common problems affecting society at large. You may also express your opinions on any everyday issue that will be of interest to the public. When you read newspapers, make it a habit to look at this column and cultivate your letter writing skills. If the editor publishes your letter, you will be encouraged to write more, and later you may start writing general or technical articles for the newspaper.

Look up newspapers and bring a letter to the editor of your choice and discuss it in class. You will learn from these examples that most letters highlight a common problem and also give solutions for consideration of the officials concerned.

Write a letter to the editor of a newspaper, discussing the major problems of road safety and suggesting practicable solutions to them. Use the official letter format.

3.4 Making Inroads

Thinking and Interaction

Discuss the following questions in pairs and share your answers with the class.

1. What are the different types of roads?

2. How are roads important to us?
3. What role do roads play in the development of a country?

Paragraph Writing

Write a paragraph of about 125 words comparing roads in villages to urban roads.

Word Power

Match the words in column A to their meanings in column B.

	A	B
1	decades	a. the number of deaths within a particular society
2	sweeping	b. to walk slowly with a lot of effort, while carrying something heavy
3	gadget	c. a feeling that makes a person want to do something
4	trudge	d. periods of ten years
5	mortality	e. affecting many things or people
6	inclination	f. a small device or machine with a particular purpose

Reading

Read the passage and answer the questions that follow.

Roads, for decades not seen in large parts of India, are actually helping improve literacy, health and quality of lives, an official study has found. More jobs, fewer child deaths, less crime, more girls in schools, changes in cropping patterns, and increased incomes for the average household—roads in India's villages have achieved all that and more, says an assessment by the Ministry of Rural Development. Sweeping changes have been observed in the lives of people in villages, which constitute 80% of the country's population. The impact assessment of the Pradhan Mantri Gram Sadak Yojana (Prime Minister's Village Road Plan) also detects unmistakable changes in the social and economic patterns of rural regions in various states, many of which had been deprived of proper roads for more than five decades.

Urbanisation has been a direct impact of rural road connectivity. Roads have drawn villagers to town entertainment, and there is greater ownership of TVs and other electrical gadgets. With roads has come cooking gas to remote villages, thus improving the lives of women who traditionally trudge long distances to collect firewood or who have to make cow dung cakes.

The states of Mizoram, Tamil Nadu and West Bengal credited roads with the conversion of temporary houses to permanent structures. With roads improving access to health facilities, there has been a decrease in infant and child mortality in Orissa, Madhya Pradesh, Himachal Pradesh, Tamil Nadu, Uttar Pradesh, and West Bengal.

School enrollment and attendance have improved in all states, it was noted, and there has been an increase in the number of girls going to school in Assam, Madhya Pradesh, Orissa, Tamil Nadu, and West Bengal. Regular attendance of teachers and a greater inclination of people to send their children to school were also attributed to roads.

The study found that roads had resulted in more jobs and self-improvement opportunities, thus improving income.

(*Source*: *The Economic Times*, 18.3.2005)

Comprehension

1. Why were roads not seen in large parts of India for many years?
2. What are the uses of roads?
3. What changes are observable in the lives of rural people?
4. What improvement is noticeable in the lives of women?
5. How did infant and child mortality come down in many states?
6. How have school enrollment and attendance increased?

Tense

Fill in the blanks with suitable tense forms of the verbs in brackets.

1. L&T Company .... (build) many IT parks in Tamil Nadu.
2. Malaysia .... (get) contracts to construct national highways in India.
3. National Highways Authority of India .... (undertake) massive efforts to improve road connectivity.
4. State Highways Department .... (step up) maintenance work of roads in the state.
5. Build, Own, Operate, and Transfer (BOOT) scheme .... (become) very popular today.

Collocation

Collocation is the way in which some words are often used together. Look at the following combinations of words.

Remote village
Sweeping changes

List some more words that go with 'remote' and 'changes'. An example for each is given for you.

remote sensing, remote ...., remote ....

drastic changes, ... changes, ... changes

Fill in the blanks with words that go with the following. The first set is given as an example.

1. home appliance, home needs, home finance
2. radio ...., ...
3. self-help ...., ...
4. infant mortality ...., ...
5. infrastructure ...., ...

Role Play

Assume that your family migrated from a village to a town many years ago. You now go to the village to attend the wedding of your cousin. You see a lot of changes in the lifestyle of the people living there. You are convinced that you could live in the village, but you have to convince your father. Two students may play these roles.

3.5 Fiber Optic Transmission

Thinking and Interaction

Discuss the following questions in pairs and share your answers with the class.

1. What is telecommunication?
2. What is the common medium of telecommunication?
3. What is fiber optic communication?

4. What are the advantages of using fiber optic cables?

Word Power

Match the words in column A to their meanings in column B.

	A	B
1	streaming	a. making a new product available for the first time
2	broadband	b. listening to or watching sound or video on a computer directly from the Internet
3	coaxial	c. a part, section, portion
4	telephony	d. the positioning or distribution of the parts of something, relative to each other
5	configuration	e. a system that enables many messages to be sent at the same time and very quickly between two computers
6	segment	f. communication by means of the telephone
7	rollout	g. having or mounted on a common axis

Reading

Read the passage and answer the questions that follow.

1. You are eagerly waiting for an important call on your landline phone but it has suddenly gone dead. This shall never happen now, as there will be no loose connections and hanging telephone cables, which get snapped every now and then. You need not visit the video library for any movie you want to see because it will now be made available to you at your convenience right on your TV screen so that you can enjoy live error-free video streaming from any remote location in the world.
2. All this may sound a little too much, but it is true. The reason for this lies in the application of a fundamental technology called fiber optic transmission.
3. Compared to conventional telecommunication, in which copper cables carry electrical signals, in fiber optic communication, optical fibers made of glass carry light signals to carry data at more than 40Gbps which is analogous to 6,25,000 voice calls running simultaneously.
4. A number of technologies have been developed to provide broadband on copper network in order to provide high data rate services like file sharing, video conferencing, video downloads, but, because of the limitations of copper cables to carry high speed data for long distances (more than 70–80m) and because of

interference due to electromagnetic fields, applications requiring high data rate transmission are not possible.

5. Today, even basic services like file sharing, online music/video sharing require large bandwidth, which cannot be provided by most of the current copper cable-based broadband networks.
6. The solution to all these problems is very simple and lies in the use of optical fibers to provide all communication services to the consumers. In a current generation home, there would be a coaxial cable for Cable TV, a twisted pair cable for telephony, and a CAT5 cable for Internet. In spite of having three different cables, the service quality is not up to the expectations. Instead, if the home is connected to all the communication networks through just one optical fiber, all the services can be provided with the highest levels of quality. This next generation system for communication is called Fiber to the Home (FTTH) or Fiber to the Premises (FTTP).
7. Fiber to the Home (FTTH) refers to a broadband telecommunications system based on fiber optic cables and associated optical electronics for delivery of multiple advanced services such as the triple play of telephone, broadband Internet, and television to homes and businesses.
8. It enables the provision of virtually unlimited bandwidth and thus all the future bandwidth intensive services would easily be provided to the users.
9. In this system, there won't be any hanging and loose untidy copper cables in your residential complex. All the service providers viz., telephone service providers, Internet service providers, and cable TV operators will terminate their cables at a central location in a residential/commercial complex and, from there, there will be just one optical fiber cable going to each home. This network is called a Passive Optical Network (PON), wherein only the opto-electronic units at the central location and in the home need electric power to operate while all the other components in the network need no electricity to run. A small device of the size of a modem is fitted in the house, which interacts between all the equipment like TVs, PCs, phones in the home, and with the external network.

10. The entire network can be managed from a remote location through the Internet, which means that nobody is physically needed in the complex to man the network. Even the service provisioning, configuration, and termination of services as per the demand of the consumers can be done remotely.
11. The FTTH has taken the world by surprise and is growing at a very rapid rate in all the developed regions like North America, the Far East Asia, and Western Europe. Nearly 50 per cent deployment of the FTTH is happening in the home segment because of increasing demand for services like video on demand, online gaming, and file sharing.
12. The FTTH rollouts have begun in India recently with many real estate developers being keen on offering the best services to their customers.
13. The major expenditure in building a new communication network is the cost of construction and deployment. Due to this, in case of a new building or complex, there is no difference in the cost of building an FTTH network and a copper network. Thus the FTTH is the logical choice for new housing. On the other side, installing an FTTH increases the property value for the home owner as it increases the future resale value of the property.

(*Source*: http://www.hindu.com/pp/2006/08/12/stories/2006081201430400.htm)

Note-taking

Complete the table with relevant information from the passage.

	Features	**Conventional telecommunication**	**Fiber optic communication**
1	medium		
2	quality of transmission		
3	speed		
4	signals		
5	bandwidth		

The Structure of a Paragraph

A paragraph is a unit of written discourse with one or more than one sentence woven around a central idea. The main idea is usually given in the topic sentence (the sentence that talks about the topic of the paragraph). This idea is further elaborated with supporting details in other sentences in the form of suitable examples, proofs, statistical details, anecdotes, etc. The paragraph normally ends with a concluding statement which rephrases the main idea powerfully.

TSC is an abbreviation that can be used to remember the structure of the paragraph.

T – Topic sentence
S – Supporting details
C – Concluding statement

The following sentences are not in proper order. Rearrange them to form a coherent paragraph.

In the current scenario, exploring energy alternatives in the form of bio-fuels, namely, ethanol and bio-diesel assumes top priority.

The current yearly consumption of diesel alone is approximately 40 million tons in India constituting about 40 per cent of all petro-products.

It is non-toxic and environment friendly as it produces substantially less carbon monoxide and the combustion gases contain no sulphur dioxide and unburnt hydrocarbons.

It can provide power similar to conventional diesel and thus can be used in diesel engines.

With the upsurge in economic activities, India is consuming over a whopping 127 million tons of crude oil a year and is forced to import about 70 per cent of its needs.

Bio-diesel, derived from the plants (bearing oils) like sunflower, canola or jatropha curcas, can be used as a substitute or an additive to diesel.

Letter to the Editor

Assume that you live in a flat. You face a number of problems with the quality of your telephone connection. You lodged a complaint with the telephone company, but the problem has not been solved. Under these circumstances, write a letter to the editor of a newspaper about the problem.

Paragraph Writing

Based on the information you have given in the table, write a paragraph of about 125 words, comparing conventional telecommunication with fiber optic communication. Remember to use the TSC structure in your paragraph.

Circular Writing

As the Secretary of the Residents' Association of your colony, prepare a circular for all residents regarding the conversion of copper cables into fiber optic cables so that no resident has any problem with the quality of communication services. In your circular, mention whether additional funds will be required and explain how the conversion process will not disrupt the lives of the residents in any way.

UNIT 4

TECHNOLOGY AND SOCIETY

4.1 Robot Soldiers

Thinking and Interaction

Discuss the following in pairs and share your answers with the class.

1. Who is a soldier?
2. What is a soldier's job?
3. Who/what is a robot soldier?
4. Why are human soldiers replaced by robot soldiers?
5. Why is Costa Rica the only country that does not have a military force?
6. Why do countries wage war with one another?
7. Is it possible for human beings to live without defence forces and wars?

Word Power

Match the words in column A to their meanings in column B.

	A	B
1	combat	a. an American
2	crucial	b. imagined as a future possibility
3	lethal	c. a person near, but not taking part, when something happens
4	bystander	d. causing death
5	envisioned	e. very important
6	Yankee	f. a fight between two people, armies, etc.

Reading

Read the two passages on robot soldiers and identify the differences between the two in terms of presentation and coverage of information. Use the table given at the end to list the differences.

Passage I

Coming Soon: Robot Soldiers

The robot soldier is coming. The Pentagon predicts that robots will be a major fighting force in the American military in less than a decade, hunting and killing enemies in combat. Robots are a crucial part of the army's effort to rebuild itself as a twenty-first century fighting force, and a $127 billion project called Future Combat Systems is the biggest military contract in American history.

The military plans to invest tens of billions of dollars in automated armed forces. The cost of that transformation will help drive the Defense Department's budget up almost 20 per cent from a requested $419.3 billion in 2010, excluding the costs of war. The annual cost of buying new weapons is scheduled to rise 50 per cent, from $78 billion to $118.6 billion.

Military planners say robot soldiers will think, see, and react increasingly like humans. In the beginning, they will be remote-controlled, looking and acting like deadly toy trucks. As the technology develops, they may take many shapes. And as their intelligence grows, so will their autonomy.

But even supporters like Robert Finklestein, President of Robotic Technology in Potomac, MD., are telling the Pentagon that it could take until 2035 to develop a robot that looks, thinks, and fights like a soldier. "The Pentagon's goal is there," he said, "but the path is not totally clear."

Already, however, several hundred robots are digging up roadside bombs in Iraq, scouring caves in Afghanistan, and serving as armed sentries at American weapons depots.

By April, an armed version of the bomb disposal robot will be in Baghdad, capable of firing 1,000 rounds a minute. Though controlled by a soldier with a laptop, the robot will be the first thinking machine of its kind to take up a front-line infantry position, ready to kill enemies.

(*Source*: *Indian Express* 17.2.2005: p. 11)

Passage II

The Yankee Robots are Coming

The US military is working on a new generation of soldiers, far different from the army it has. "They don't get hungry," said Gordon Johnson of the Pentagon's Joint Forces

Command. "They're not afraid. They don't forget their orders. They don't care if the guy next to them has just been shot. Will they do a better job than human beings? Yes."

The robot soldier is coming. The Pentagon predicts that robots will be a major fighting force in the American military in less than a decade, hunting and killing enemies in combat. Robots are a crucial part of the army's effort to rebuild itself as a twenty-first century fighting force, and $127 billion project called Future Combat Systems is the biggest military contract in American history.

The military plans to invest tens of billions of dollars in armed forces. The costs of that transformation will drive the Defense Department's budget up almost 20 per cent. Military planners say robot soldiers will think, see, and react increasingly like humans. In the beginning, they will be remote-controlled, looking and acting much like lethal toy trucks. As the technology develops, they may take many shapes. And as their intelligence grows, so will their autonomy.

The robot soldier has been a dream at the Pentagon for 30 years. And some involved in the work say it may take at least 30 more years to realise in full. Well before then, they say, the military will have to answer some tough questions if it intends to trust robots with the responsibility of distinguishing friend from foe, combatant from innocent bystander.

Even the strongest advocates of automatons say that war will always remain a human endeavour, marked by death and disaster. And supporters are telling the Pentagon that it could take until 2035 to develop a robot that looks, thinks, and fights like a soldier.

Robots in battle, as envisioned by their builders, may look and move like humans or hummingbirds, tractors or tanks, cockroaches or crickets. With the development of nanotechnology—the science of very small structures—they may become swarms of "smart dust". The Pentagon intends for robots to haul munitions, gather intelligence, search buildings, or blow them up.

All these are in the works, but not yet in battle. Already, however, several hundred robots are digging up roadside bombs in Iraq, scouring caves in Afghanistan, and serving as armed sentries at American weapon depots. By April, an armed version of the bomb disposal robot will be in Baghdad, capable of firing 1000 rounds a minute. Controlled by a soldier with a laptop, the robot will be the first thinking machine of its kind to take up a front-line infantry position, ready to kill enemies.

"The American military will have these kinds of robots," Mr. Johnson said. "It's not a question of if; it's a question of when."

(*Source*: *The Hindu Newscape* 17.2.2005: p. 22.)

Comprehension

1. What do you learn by comparing the two passages?
2. Which passage appeals to you? Give reasons for your answer.

Complete the following table.

	Reading Passage I	Reading Passage II
Presentation		
Coverage		
Appeal		

Word Origin: Latin

Look at the following words.

combat
crucial
military
invest
transformation
annual
schedule

These words are derived from the Latin language, which has given a lot of words to the English language. One of the wonderful qualities of Latin, like Greek, is that it helps English to make many more new words and add them to its stock.

The root of '*combat*' is '*battere*' which means to fight. This root is found in words like *battle*, *acrobat*, etc. The prefix '*com-*' means '*with*', so '*combat*' means '*to fight with*'.

Find out the prefix, root, suffix, and meaning of each of the following root words. Add more words of the same root to the word. An example for each is given.

	Word	Prefix	Root	Suffix	Meaning	Examples
1	crucial	--	crux	-ial	cross	crucifixion, crucible, crux,
2	military					
3	invest					
4	transformation					
5	annual					
6	schedule					

Go back to Unit 1.1 which deals with the English language. Carefully read the passage again. You will find that most of the words used to describe English have their roots in Latin. Here is a list of those words.

original, invader, influence, addition, century, renaissance, vocabulary, missionary, hospitality

Note-taking

Complete the table using information available in the two passages. You may add any other interesting points of your own.

	Human soldier	Robot soldier
Advantages		
1.		
2.		
3.		

(Contd...)

4.		
Disadvantages		
1.		
2.		
3.		
4.		

Paragraph Writing

Using the information from the table, write a paragraph of about 125 words comparing the human soldier with the robot soldier.

Role Play

Imagine that you are a soldier working with a robot soldier in a battlefield. You are wounded by a shot from the enemy and you become unconscious. Surprisingly, the robot soldier you work with saves you by taking you to the military hospital on time. Now enter into a conversation with the robot soldier and find out what happened to you and how you were saved.

Personal Letter Writing

Imagining you are a wounded soldier, write a letter to your mother about how you were saved by a robot soldier.

Food for Thought

"Science without conscience is nescience."

4.2 For a Snapshot of the Web

Thinking and Interaction

Discuss the following questions in pairs and share your answers with the class.

1. What is the Internet?
2. Who invented the Internet?
3. What are the common uses of the Internet?
4. What are the educational uses of the Internet?
5. What are the difficulties in using the Internet?

Word Power

Match the words in column A to their meanings in column B.

	A	B
1	furnished with	a. a photograph
2	snapshot	b. points at which one can make no further progress in work
3	contend	c. not connected to the internet
4	offline	d. provided with
5	dead ends	e. to struggle in order to overcome a competitor

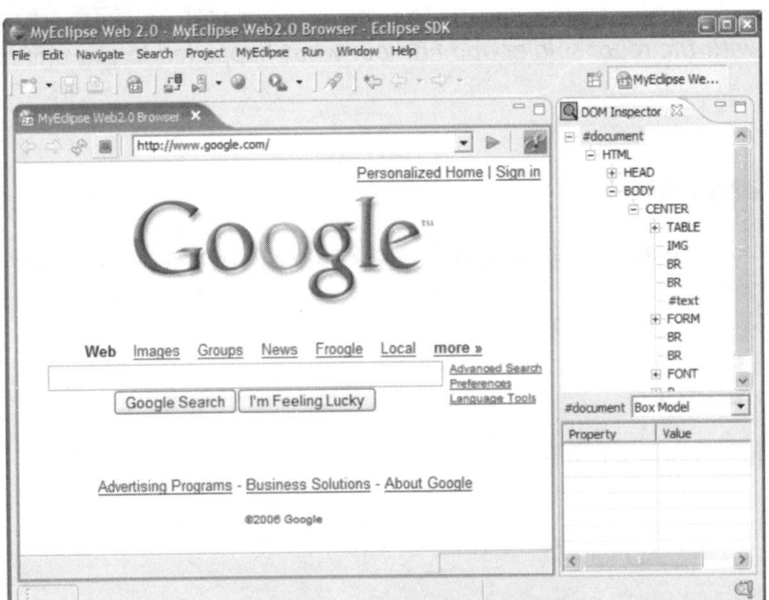

Listening

Listen to a short talk titled 'For a Snapshot of the Web' and answer the following questions.

1. *Choose the correct answer.*

   a) Which is the newest company?
      i) Google
      ii) Yahoo
      iii) Microsoft
      iv) Webaroo

   b) Content density means ....
      i) giving the essential information
      ii) giving all information
      iii) giving the information required by the user
      iv) giving additional information to the user

   c) The servers of Webaroo scan the Internet for ....
      i) quantity, coverage, and length
      ii) quality, coverage, and size
      iii) length, width, and depth
      iv) access, use, and coverage

   d) The system updates itself to ....
      i) get new information
      ii) throw old information out
      iii) make itself new
      iv) include necessary information

2. *State whether the following statements are true or false.*

   a) Webaroo plans to open up a new facility for Internet users.
   b) According to Brad Husick, the Internet is always difficult to use.
   c) Webaroo has set up many data centers.
   d) Web users go through all pages given by search engines.
   e) Webaroo is set up by an Indian and an American.
   f) All information on the Web is useful.

3. *Choose the appropriate meaning for the given words and phrases as they are used in the talk.*

   a) legions

   i) swarm
   ii) a unit of the ancient Roman army
   iii) lords
   iv) great numbers

b) fledgling
   i) recently formed organisation
   ii) orphaned
   iii) dynamic
   iv) well-known

c) access
   i) assessment
   ii) data
   iii) reachability
   iv) utility

d) redundancy
   i) abundance
   ii) repetition
   iii) great use
   iv) frequency

e) strive
   i) try hard
   ii) strengthen
   iii) succeed
   iv) hope

f) frustration
   i) unhappiness
   ii) effort
   iii) fright
   iv) disappointment

Paragraph Writing

Write a paragraph of about 125 words on the importance of making up-to-date information available to the people through the Internet.

4.3 Mobile Phone Menace

Thinking and Interaction

Discuss the following questions in pairs and share your answers with the class.

1. What is a menace?
2. How is the mobile phone a menace today?
3. How do people misuse mobile phones?
4. How can we stop the mobile phone from becoming a menace?
5. What are the common problems of technological advancements?

Word Power

Match the following words and phrases in column A to their meanings in column B.

	A	B
1	recalcitrant	a. planned ways of doing something
2	contorted	b. calmly and carelessly
3	nonchalantly	c. to knock or strike somebody with a short hard push
4	tactics	d. resisting discipline and authority
5	bump into	e. twisted out of natural shape

Reading

Read the passage and answer the following questions.

Campaign against use of mobile phones while driving is hardly making a dent among the recalcitrant two wheeler riders.

Pedestrians lost in a conversation even while crossing busy road stretches, two wheeler riders holding the instrument between a contorted shoulder and the ear, and auto and share auto drivers nonchalantly indulging in a mobile phone conversation while driving with a vehicle full of passengers are putting several people on the road to serious threat.

If holding the phone with a hand or shoulder or talking through a hand-free earpiece is difficult, motorcyclists employ other tactics such as sticking the phone through the helmet or asking a pillion rider to hold the phone as the rider speaks while driving.

More than violating traffic rules by using the phone, motorcyclists say that those who use mobile phones often get mentally transported away from the road that they are not even aware if they bump into someone because of their lack of concentration.

(*Source*: "Reporter's Diary", *The Hindu*, 11.4.2006, p. 3)

Comprehension

1. What is the main idea of the passage?
2. Why are several people on roads put to serious threat?
3. What are the techniques used by motorcyclists to use their mobile phones?
4. What are the main problems with motorcyclists?

Group Discussion

Mobile phone menace in public places, or even in private places, is a common problem that all of us are faced with. In groups of four or five, discuss this problem, come up with a few practicable solutions, and the group leader may report the solutions to the class.

Tense

Fill in the blanks with suitable tense forms of the verbs given in brackets.

I .... (happen) to travel by auto one day, when it suddenly .... (jerk) to a halt. The driver .... (get) a call on his mobile. I .... (did) not .... (grudge) him the time till I .... (realise) he .... (discuss) the *bajjis* that he .... (eat) at his friend's house. Angry, I .... (ask) him to resume his conversation later. I .... (be) taken aback when he .... (turn) around and .... (accuse) me of being impatient!

4.4 Knowledge Society

Thinking and Interaction

Discuss the following questions in pairs and share your answers with the class.

1. What is a society?

2. What is a knowledge society?
3. In which society do we live now?
4. How can we develop our society into a full-fledged knowledge society?

Word Power

Match the words in column A to their meanings in column B.

	A	B
1	perception	a. the state of being near something
2	occurrence	b. controlling and using
3	proximity	c. the process of making clear and definite
4	archiving	d. a person who reaches truths beyond human understanding
5	retrieving	e. the ability to see, hear or understand things
6	harnessing	f. to store electronic information that you no longer need to use regularly
7	globalisation	g. irregular curves or surfaces produced by repeated subdivisions
8	crystallisation	h. finding and bringing back something
9	fractals	i. an event, an incident
10	mystic	j. free movement of goods and services making society and culture similar in all parts of the world

Reading

Read the passage and answer the following questions.

A knowledge society is a formal association of people with similar interests, who try to make effective use of their combined knowledge about their areas of interest, and in the process contribute to this knowledge. In this sense, knowledge is the psychological and useful result of perception, learning, and reasoning.

Knowledge societies have the characteristic that knowledge forms the major component of any activity, particularly economic activities. Economic, social, cultural, and all other human activities become dependent on a huge volume of knowledge and information. A knowledge society/economy is one in which knowledge becomes a major product and raw material.

Knowledge societies are not a new occurrence. For example, fishermen have long shared the knowledge of predicting the weather to their community, and this knowledge gets added to the social capital of the community. What is new is that with current technologies, knowledge societies need not be constrained by geographic proximity. Current technology offers much more possibilities for sharing, archiving, and retrieving knowledge. Knowledge has become the most important capital in the present age, and hence the success of any society lies in harnessing it.

Knowledge and information are vital components of the formation of any society because every society is formed around some shared concepts. One of the contributions of Globalisation and new ICT is creation of a global society with a shared knowledge of issues and possibilities.

'Material resources and their processing'—henceforth *E*—have been the basis of economic growth. Music, art, path-breaking thought streams, mixing of cultural attributes of different societies bringing in new cultural attributes, etc.,—henceforth *C*—result in cultural development and act as a catalyst in entire social development. Now that the many societies have so matured that almost all the activities involved in E and C rely very much on the existing knowledge base. This knowledge is available in written documents, written laws, unwritten laws, people's convictions, people's words in different languages, etc.

In the same way, as the unequal distribution of materials (wealth in generalised term) caused unbalanced and inappropriate development of society to date, imbalances in the knowledge distribution, knowledge availability, knowledge sharing, etc., hinder the economic/cultural/social development of human societies. The knowledge societies first realise the importance of knowledge and also the importance of proper knowledge distribution, sharing and building for social development.

Knowledge by nature is free. It should be free for better benefit of society. It should be free for better development and crystallisation of knowledge. The argument that freeing knowledge kills motivation for creating knowledge should be addressed.

People from the same field—teachers teaching the same subject, fans of the same musical group, and artists with similar interests—and people from different fields—engineers talking to scientists about a scientific issue related to their engineering project, researchers of different fields discussing a common research problem, artists interested in fractals getting in touch with programmers, and mystics talking to scientists—should happen frequently.

A knowledge society needs infrastructure like i) physical: meeting places, notice boards and ii) technological: local language content sharing, mailing lists, web portals, wikis, chat rooms, video conferencing, virtual meetings, collaborative development environments, and distance education. Free software movement is a success story of knowledge society.

(*Source*: http://en.wikipedia.org/wiki/Knowledge_society)

Understanding Summary

Answer the following questions.

1. What is a summary?
2. What are its uses?
3. What are the many other terms which are associated with summary?
4. How are these other terms used in different contexts for different purposes?
5. Where is the term 'skills summary' used?

Summary Writing

Summarise the passage in about 100 words. First prepare a rough draft. Revise it and then write the fair draft.

Understanding Compound Nouns

Look at the following terms.

robot soldiers, Yankee robots, computer science

These three terms have more than one noun. Groups of nouns like these are called compound nouns. You will come across such compound nouns in your professional and daily life. Read them carefully and understand their meanings. For example, 'computer science' can be explained as a science of computers. Compound nouns may have more than two nouns. For example, *Software Technology Park*, *File Transfer Protocol*, *Database Management System*, etc.

Give definitions for the following compound nouns.

Service provider
Phone menace
Knowledge society
Information technology
Management science
Research station
Control board
World peace
Space administration
Knowledge worker

Look at the following phrases.

One who organises programmes
A corporation that deals with power

These phrases can be changed into the compound nouns listed below.

A programme organiser
A power corporation

Change the following phrases into compound nouns.

A branch of engineering that deals with transportation
A branch of science that is concerned with information
A field of engineering that deals with software
A technology that is devoted to textiles
A science about polymers
A planet which is a dwarf

Word Power

Learn the meanings of the words given in the box and fill in the blanks with suitable words from the box.

maintaining, fluctuation, architects, façade, vents, labyrinth, criterion, virtuosities, notorious, orientation, mounds, branch, ventilators, drift, avowed, energy, corrugated, subterranean, atriums, towers, bio-mimicking, thermoregulation, celebrated, technology, diurnal

Termites are .... for their destructive effect on buildings. But do you know that they can teach us a lesson or two in .... temperatures inside buildings in an eco-friendly manner?

Magnetic Termites found in Australia and Macrotermes Bellicosus in Africa build large .... Some of them rise to a height of 7.5m. In spite of the high .... in external temperature, the internal temperature of the African termite .... is maintained well. Sometimes the fluctuation may be in the order of 10°C to 44°C.

There is a .... of science called bio-mimicry that studies nature and adapts it for engineering and design applications. Janine Benyus, ... biologist from the U.S., made the term bio-mimicry popular. In Janine's view the .... objective of mimicking is not to extract from nature but to learn from it. Learning from termite activity is one aspect of this science.

Termites control temperature by building thick outer walls and air .... The outer wall is made up of a mix of mud and saliva. This is a very strong material and the local people use it for building houses and even to lay roads.

The .... of the tower helps wind drive air through the tower. The air mixes with the water droplets brought by the termites from the .... and rises through the central passage. When the outside temperature is hot, all air vents are kept open and air is allowed to .... When the temperature outside is low and the air cold, obstacles are built along the passages to block the draft. This helps to keep the inside temperature hot. This .... is impressive and designers have tried to adopt it for efficient air-conditioning of buildings.

Mick Pearce is one of the early .... who adopted this termite behavior to design the East Gate office complex and shopping mall in Harare, Zimbabwe. The architect first limited the glass .... to 25 per cent. A simple device was invented. Fresh air from outside was sucked through the .... using fans. It circulated through hollow spaces under the floors and into the rooms through baseboard .... The air then is drawn through many brick funnels on the roof. During cooler nights, fans circulate air through the building and flush the stored heat in the building to the cooler surrounding outside. This has helped the building use less than 10 per cent of the .... of a conventional building its size.

.... is a variation of this principle and is designed by Atelier Ten—environmental engineers, London and it is used in the Federation Square, Melbourne. It is a maze of zig-zag .... concrete walls. It uses the .... temperature variations to provide a passive cooling system. In the night, cool air is pumped in and the concrete cooled. During the day, air is pumped again through the labyrinth and the concrete cools it in turn. This cooled air then flows to the atrium.

In Janine Benyus' words, ... has to be measured in terms of "how well-adapted it is to life on earth over the long term". Going by this ...., one may find that many of our designs are yet to be adapted well. They may be technological .... But the question is: what do they mean in the long term? The hope here is that .... would offer a route to innovative and adaptive technologies.

(*Source*: http://www.hindu.com/pp/2006/02/25/stories/2006022500090500.htm)

Insight

How many blanks were you able to fill in without much difficulty? If you understand the context and the overall meaning of the passage, you can easily choose the correct words.

> The more frequently you communicate in a language, the more your active vocabulary increases. You must develop your vocabulary by constantly communicating in all four forms—listening, speaking, reading, and writing.

Food for Thought

"No grammar, some communication: no words, no communication."

Paragraph Writing

Write a paragraph of about 125 words on why world governments are interested in making their countries knowledge societies.

4.5 Nanotechnology

Thinking and Interaction

Discuss the following questions in pairs and share your answers with the class.

1. What are the major thrust areas of scientific research today?
2. Why are scientists and technologists making things smaller and smaller?
3. What is the science and technology of very small structures?
4. How are such small structures useful to us?
5. What is a podcast and what are its uses?

Word Power

Match the words in Column A to their meanings in Column B.

	A	B
1	notorious	a. involving the use of new discoveries, methods, or ideas
2	replicate	b. able to destroy naturally without harming the environment

(Contd...)

3	semiconductor	c. well-known for some bad quality
4	diagnostic	d. able to continue over a period of time
5	biodegradable	e. to make something necessary
6	sustainable	f. a material which allows electricity to move through it more easily when its temperature increases
7	ground-breaking	g. of finding the exact nature of a disease
8	entail	h. make or do something again in exactly the same way

Reading

Read the passage and answer the questions that follow.

Viruses are notorious villains. They cause serious human diseases like AIDS, polio, and influenza, and can lead to system crashes and data loss in computers.

A new podcast explores how nanotechnology researcher Angela Belcher, from Massachusetts Institute of Technology (MIT), is working with viruses to make them do good things. By exploiting a virus's ability to replicate rapidly and combine with semiconductor and electronic materials, she is coaxing them to grow and self-assemble nanomaterials into a functional electronic device. Through this marriage of nanotechnology with green chemistry, Belcher and her team are working toward building faster, better, cheaper and environmentally-friendly transistors, batteries, solar cells, diagnostic materials for detecting cancer, and semiconductors for use in modern electrical devices—everything from computers to cell phones.

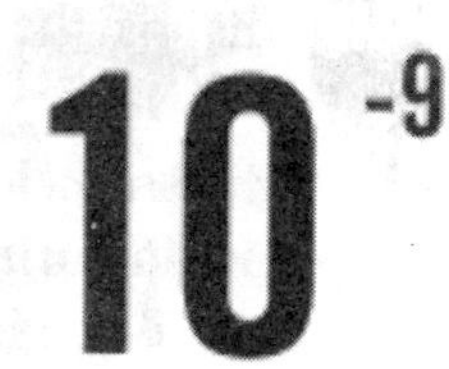

Unlike traditional semiconductor or battery manufacturing which requires expensive and toxic chemicals, Belcher's nanofactories generate little waste, grow at room temperature, and promise to be inexpensive and largely biodegradable. Does all this sound too good to be true? Judge for yourself.

"Nanotechnology is the future. In 2006 alone, governments, corporations, and venture capitalists spent $12 billion on nanotechnology research and development worldwide. It promises to change just about everything—our medical care, energy sources, communications and food. It is leading us to what many in government and industry are calling 'The Next Industrial Revolution.' Society needs to prepare now for how to exploit and harness its potential, especially to ensure that nanotechnology makes possible a greener, more sustainable tomorrow," said David Rejeski, Director of the Project on Emerging Nanotechnologies at the Wilson Center.

"Dr Belcher's research with viruses, proteins and yeast offers hope for new, ground-breaking solutions to the world's energy problems. It holds out the prospect of using nanotechnology in a variety of ways, ranging from improving the efficiency of production, storage, and transmission of energy to overcoming many of the obstacles to a hydrogen-based transportation system based on fuel-cell powered cars and trucks," according to Rejeski.

Nanotechnology entails the measurement, prediction and construction of materials on the scale of atoms and molecules. A nanometer is one-billionth of a metre, and nanotechnology typically deals with particles and structures larger than 1 nanometre, but smaller than 100 nanometres. To put this into perspective, the width of a human hair is approximately 80,000 nanometres. It is estimated that $2.6 trillion in manufactured goods will incorporate nanotech, or about 15 per cent of total global output in 2014.

(*Source*: www.sciencedaily.com)

Comprehension

1. Why are viruses described as villains?
2. What is the unique characteristic of viruses?
3. What do you understand by the term 'green chemistry'?
4. What is the outcome of the bringing together of nanotechnology and green chemistry?
5. Why are Belcher's nanofactories superior to traditional semiconductor or battery manufacturing?
6. Why does David Rejeski strongly believe that 'nanotechnology is the future'?
7. How is nanotechnology related to the Industrial Revolution?
8. How can Belcher's research be useful in solving the world's energy problems?
9. How is nanotechnology defined?
10. What example is given for the concept of nanometre?

Disyllabic Prefixes

Look at the prefixes '*ultra*'– and '*nano*–'. '*Ultra*' means extreme or extremely and '*nano*' means 'of microscopic size' or 'a thousand millionth' i.e., 10^{-9}.

Give at least five words each with 'ultra' and 'nano' as prefixes.

Here are a few more disyllabic prefixes with examples. Think of at least three words for each of them. One example for each prefix has been given.

Auto – automobile
Cyber – cybernetics

Eco – ecofriendly
Giga – gigawatt
Hyper – hyperactive
Inter – Internet
Mega – megabyte
Micro – microscope
Multi – multi-tasking
Para – paralinguistic
Photo – photosynthesis
Semi – semi-circle
Super – superconductivity
Tele – telecommunication
Under – underprivileged

Word Power

Fill in the blanks with suitable disyllabic prefixes.

1. Chennai has several .... mobile industries.
2. India and other countries promote .... tourism.
3. Solar cells are also called .... voltaic cells.
4. Today people use more cell phones than .... phones.
5. Some courses of study related to medicine are called as .... medical courses.

Definition Writing

When you want to describe something accurately, you must choose your words with care so that there is no place for misunderstanding. For example, look at definition of knowledge society given below.

> 'A knowledge society is a formal association of people with similar interests, who try to make effective use of their combined knowledge about their areas of interest, and in the process contribute to this knowledge.'

For another example, look at the definition of a catalyst given below.

> 'A catalyst is a substance that makes a chemical reaction happen faster without being changed.'

A formula for definition writing can be arrived at from the above definitions: $a+b+c=d$, wherein a is the term defined, b is the class to which the term belongs, c is the special characteristic or use of the term, and d is the definition.

You can apply this formula to any good definition.

This kind of definition is usually a single sentence. If the definition exceeds more than a sentence, it becomes an extended definition and takes the form of a paragraph.

Define the following terms.

1. robot
2. technology
3. biotechnology
4. Internet
5. satellite
6. mobile phone
7. chat room
8. battery
9. zinc oxide
10. laptop

Understanding Punctuation Marks

Punctuation marks play a vital role in written communication. They attempt to correspond to some intonation patterns and speech habits in oral communication. Accurate and clear communication is made possible through good use of punctuation.

Here is a table showing the relationship between intonation patterns and habits in speech and punctuation marks in writing. There may not be actual correspondence between the two points given together, but they give an idea of the similarity.

	Intonation patterns and habits in speech	**Punctuation marks in writing**
1	rising tone	question mark
2	falling tone	period (full stop)
3	mild pause	comma
4	strong pause	colon, semi-colon
5	strong emotions	exclamation mark
6	diversion from the main topic	parenthesis, dashes
7	emphasis	underline, italics, bold
8	omitted words	ellipsis

Go back to the passage on nanotechnology in unit 4.5 and see how various punctuation marks have been used in the passage.

Punctuate the following passage.

as soldiers fired bursts from m 16 rifles at an urban warfare training site a group of college students gathered on the edge of a small runway nearby to demonstrate the latest advances in aerial robotics an emerging technology that could save lives in combat or natural disasters

some of the diminutive aircraft resembled the single engine model planes flown by hobbyists on weekends but they were packed with computer gadgetry video cameras and satellite guidance systems others were miniature helicopters and some were totally out of the box such as a yellow four propeller craft resembling a hovercraft a creation of students at the college of engineering in delhi.

all of them were programmed to accomplish their tasks on their own without any remote control manipulation by human controllers they differ from other unmanned aircraft such as the predator and global hawk which must be guided by people.

sponsored by the association for unmanned vehicle systems international of arlington virginia the competition attracts college students from around the world who design and build the planes flown during the annual three day competition at fort benning

Food for Thought

"Punctuation and punctuality go together."

Personal Letter Writing

Assume that your friend is interested in nanotechnology. He/she wants to pursue his/her higher education in the field of nanotechnology. Write a letter to your friend about the research work of Angela Belcher and ask him/her to contact this researcher for advice and help in pursuing higher studies at the Massachusetts Institute of Technology.

UNIT 5

TRAVEL AND TOURISM

5.1 Man's Desire for Travel

Thinking and Interaction

Discuss the following questions in pairs and share your answers with the class.

1. Why do people travel?
2. What problems do people commonly face while travelling?
3. How do physically challenged people travel?
4. What do you know about Helen Keller and Stephen Hawking?
5. How can trains, buses, airplanes, and other modes of transport be friendly to the physically challenged?

Word Power

Match the words in column A to their meanings in column B.

	A	B
1	at random	a. done without advance preparation
2	spas	b. big and strong
3	burly	c. without conscious choice
4	impromptu	d. those who treat sick people depending on faith and prayer alone
5	faith healers	e. springs of mineral water considered to be healthy to drink

Reading

Given below is a letter from a physically challenged person. Read the letter and answer the questions that follow.

The Spirit of Travel by Mavis Hobbs

Dear Other Disabled Travellers,

Kylee and I flew to Rotorua, which we just picked at random because it's an ideal place to take in the thermal baths, spas, etc.

Having motor neuron disease, I am very limited with my legs and either use a wheelchair or a walking wheelie to get around. The plane trip from Melbourne was smooth sailing. There was no-fuss assistance getting to my seat or the toilets with the help of an in-cabin wheelchair. Preparation beforehand is essential.

Luckily, I had a fun loving young friend. Everywhere we went (with me in a travelling lightweight wheelchair), we were greeted with friendliness. We even went on a wet and wild safari trekking tour in a 4×4 wheel drive run by a burly Maori chief, who put me on his shoulders when the going was rough.

I recommend just having a go at travelling, disability, and all. Keep a sense of humour and surround yourself with happy, fun loving people. Driving around was fine; we never had difficulty finding a ground floor motel room with cooking facilities, and friendly hotel managers provided a plastic chair for my shower. Be flexible. When Kylee went dancing in Auckland, TV and chatting in the lounge were fun in themselves for me. I am planning more impromptu trips overseas.

In the four years since my disabling disease, I have travelled to Brazil twice to visit the many faith healers. I wasn't cured, but the journey to loving, caring groups of diverse people was quite an adventure. I now see how people live from a different angle as compared to my totally mobile and active days of past years! My advice is "Do it now and have no regrets later!"

From a happy disabled traveller, Mavis Hobbs.

(*Source*:http://globalaccessnews.com/spiritoftravel.htm)

Comprehension

1. How did Mavis Hobbs become disabled?
2. How does Mavis describe her friend Kylee?
3. What did the Maori chief do for Mavis?
4. What did Mavis do when Kylee went dancing?
5. Why did Mavis visit Brazil?
6. What did Mavis learn from her travel experience?
7. What is Mavis's advice to other disabled travellers?
8. What is Ms Hobbs' nationality?

Asking Questions

Imagine that you are a journalist who happens to meet Ms Hobbs in India. What are the questions that you would like to ask her? List at least five questions.

Understanding People

There are different kinds of people with different abilities and aptitudes. We should be aware of the needs and problems of the people around us. Effective communication starts with a good understanding of one's own self and those we are communicating with.

Word Power

1. *Read through the passage and fill in the blanks with suitable words.*

A visually .... British adventurer touched down in Sydney on 1st May 2007 to end an epic 21,725-km flight by microlight aircraft from London. Miles Hilton-Barber, a 58-year-old father of three, braved snowstorms, freezing temperatures, and torrential downpours during his 54-day .... under the supervision of a sighted .... Richard Meredith-Hardy (46).

"It's the .... of an amazing dream," Mr. Hilton-Barber told reporters at Sydney's Bankstown airport. "I've wanted to be a .... since I was a kid. Now I'm totally blind and I've had the .... of flying more than halfway around the world," he said. Mr. Hilton-Barber, who lost his eyesight to a hereditary .... about 20 years ago, is hoping the trip will raise $2.5 million (Australian) for the charity Seeing is Believing, which works for the .... of blindness in developing countries.

He .... the skies from Biggin Hill air base in south London on March 7 in a microlight aircraft—which looks like a cross between a tricycle and a motorised hang-glider—with the .... of an audio device that reads out .... information such as air speed and altitude.

Mr. Hilton-Barber has also .... Mount Kilimanjaro and Mont Blanc, run marathons in the Sahara and Gobi deserts, and even .... to reach the South Pole, hauling a sledge over 400 km of Antarctic ice.

(*Source*: http://www.hindu.com/2007/05/01/stories/2007050103181300.htm)

2. *Look at the words in the box below. If the words correspond to the answers you have provided, pat yourself on the back for your excellent word power.*

co-pilot, privilege, prevention, navigational, attempted, journey, pilot, disabled, took, conquered, fulfillment, braved, condition, aid

Insight

Do you see the indomitable spirit of the man that flies in the sky without eyesight? What cannot even be thought of is made possible by the willing and the hard working.

5.2 The Great Indian Globetrotter

Thinking and Interaction

Discuss the following questions in pairs and share your answers with the class.

1. What is diaspora?
2. What is the Indian diaspora?
3. Who is a globetrotter?
4. How is globetrotting made easy now?
5. Why do you Indians travel abroad more frequently than before?

Word Power

Match the words in column A to their meanings in column B.

	A	B
1	ubiquitous	a. a thing to which more respect or attention is given than is normal

(Contd...)

2	bungee jumping	b. combined neatly
3	fetish	c. seeming to be everywhere or in several places at the same time
4	dove-tailed	d. leading
5	ardently	e. the sport of jumping off a very high bridge or similar structure, with a long elastic rope tied to your legs so that the rope pulls you back before you hit the ground
6	spearheading	f. enthusiastically

Listening

Listen to a short talk titled 'The Indian Globetrotter' and attempt the following exercises.

Note-taking

Fill in the blanks in the notes given below.

1. Ubiquitous Indian Globetrotter
   Present everywhere: ....
   .... went abroad in .... jump over
   .... mark ....
2. The Great Indian Middle Class:
   Facilitators: money, ..., ...

	Survey conducted by	Amount spent by Indian travellers
1		
2		
3		
4		
5		
6		
7		
8		

3. Competitive offers
   a. Airliners ....
   b. Countries and cities ....
4. Entry of China
   a. Malaysia's Truly Asia campaign ....

b. Uniquely Singapore Campaign ....
....
c. Unlikeliest countries ....
....
d. Australian Tourism ....
....

5. Old and new diaspora
a. Old breed ....
....
b. New breed ....
....
c. Famous places frequented by old Indian travellers ....
....

Comprehension

1. What is the connection between the Indian globetrotter and the diaspora?
2. What factors have helped the Indian middle class travel globally?
3. How does advertising help in promoting tourism?
4. Why do even smaller countries seriously engage in promoting tourism?
5. Why does the Indian traveller feel at home anywhere in the world?

Symbols of some world currencies are given in the second column. Write out the names and the countries of these currencies in the first and third columns, respectively.

	Currency	Symbol	Country/countries
1		Rs	
2		$	
3		£	
4		€	
5		P	
6		¥	
7		Fr	

(Contd...)

8		DM	
9		K	
10		руб	

Descriptive Writing

Imagine that you visited a place of tourist interest. Write a paragraph on your travel experience and what you learnt from it.

5.3 First Woman Tourist in Space

Thinking and Interaction

Discuss the following questions in pairs and share your answers with the class

1. What is space tourism?
2. Who are some of the space tourists you have heard about?
3. Which country has aggressively promoted space tourism?
4. Why are some countries interested in promoting space tourism?

Word Power

Match the words in column A to their meanings in column B.

	A	B
1	cosmodrome	a. a group of people sent to space
2	entrepreneur	b. on or in a spacecraft
3	mission	c. Russian spacecraft launching station
4	onboard	d. a person who starts a commercial business taking financial risks

Reading

Read the passage and answer the questions that follow.

Anousheh Ansari has become the first female tourist to visit space. Taking off from the Baikonur Cosmodrome in Kazakhstan onboard a Soyuz TMA spacecraft this morning,

Ms Ansari joined the Expedition 14 crew on their ten-day mission to the International Space Station. As a successful entrepreneur and co-founder of a telecommunications company, Ms Ansari is thought to have paid Space Adventures $20 million (£11 million) to join the mission. Speaking ahead of the shuttle's launch, the US businesswoman described it as a "once in a lifetime opportunity." "Exploring the cosmos has been a dream of mine that I have kept in my heart starting from a young age and I am very fortunate now to be able to actually experience it," Ms Ansari said. "Through this mission I want to create awareness of the sciences and, specifically, space exploration. I also want to share the experience with as many as possible, so that people from all over the world will know how it feels to fly in the Earth's orbit." Before she could join the shuttle's crew, Ms Ansari had to complete a cosmonaut training program at the Yuri Gagarin Cosmonaut Training Centre in the aptly-named Star City in Russia. As well as Ms. Ansari, the Expedition 14 crew includes NASA astronaut Michael Lopez-Alegria and Russian cosmonaut Mikhail Tyurin.

(*Source*: http://www.grant-thornton.co.uk/pages/press_room-other_news-first_woman_tourist_in_space.html)

Comprehension

1. Who is Ms Ansari?
2. What is the current Indian value of a US dollar?
3. Approximately how much money in Indian rupees did Ms Ansari pay to Space Adventures?
4. What was her childhood dream?
5. Why did Ms Ansari undergo a cosmonaut training program?

Understanding Infinitives

Look at the italicised words in the following sentences.

1. Anousheh Ansari has become the first female tourist *to visit* space.
2. Ms Ansari is thought to have paid Space Adventures $20 million (£11 million) *to join* the mission.
3. I am very fortunate now to be able *to actually experience* it.

4. I also want *to share* the experience with as many as possible, so that people from all over the world will know how it feels *to fly* in the Earth's orbit.
5. Ms Ansari had *to complete* a cosmonaut training program.

An infinitive is the basic form of a verb used preceded by '*to*', which is the infinitive marker. This '*to*' is different from the preposition '*to*'. The infinitive can occur in all tense forms.

Purpose Statements

The infinitive form is often used to refer to the purpose or aim of someone or something. For example, Anousheh Ansari's desire was *to visit* space. Similarly, objects and tools have certain purposes and uses. Look at the examples given below.

The purpose of a spacecraft is *to travel* in space.

The aim of a cosmodrome is *to launch* spacecrafts into space.

Write purpose statements for the following.

1. Aircraft: to transport travellers from one place to another via air
2. Airport: to land and take off aircrafts safely
3. Train: to transport people over railway tracks
4. Railway station: to send and receive trains in stations
5. Rocket: to carry satellites into space
6. Launch pad: to send off rockets.

Punctuation

Punctuate the following passage.

the east coast road ecr is no doubt one of the finest roads in India but it is not the safest one for travel the traffic authorities have put up barricades in several places to reduce the speed of the vehicles this may be effective in controlling speeding vehicles but it is very dangerous no one can deny that several accidents take place due to the barricades

there are two reasons for this one there is no signboard indicating that there are barricades ahead and two there is no proper lighting where the barricades are put up

sometimes the barricades hit by some vehicles are left as they are in the middle of the road will the traffic authorities take notice of this and set things in order

5.4 Travel as Discovery

Thinking and Interaction

Discuss the following questions in pairs and share your answers with the class.

1. What relates travel with discovery?
2. What do travellers learn from their journeys?
3. How does travel help us understand life better?
4. How has travel helped some scientists gather data for their path breaking studies?

Word Power

Match the words in column A to their meanings in column B.

	A	B
1	suffocates	a. cruel or unfair
2	oppressive	b. causes difficulty in breathing
3	engendered	c. spending very little money
4	shoestring	d. caused a situation or condition
5	gaunt	e. not visited or seen by many
6	secluded	f. (of a person) made exceptionally thin
7	inarticulate	g. sharing or exchanging the same thoughts or feelings
8	communion	h. unable to express one's ideas or feelings very clearly
9	sublimity	i. recording
10	logging	j. being extremely good, beautiful or enjoyable

Reading

Read the passage and answer the questions that follow.

Travel wields a great power; the traveller often falls in love with travelling. For me, travel is a kind of narcotic and antidote. Seoul's atmosphere suffocates me. I have to travel to free myself from this oppressive feeling engendered by city life.

We, the members of the Youth Hostel Association, travel on shoestring budgets. Travelling with such little money makes some difficulties inevitable. After any one of my journeys, my face is deeply tanned and looking a bit gaunt due to excessive exercise and modest eating. I am utterly worn out and exceedingly tired. But, each of my journeys supplies me with a host of beautiful memories and reflections.

When we went to the secluded Kariwang Mt., we climbed all night and found secret springs between the rocks to quench our thirst. Such pure spring water moves me. Last year we journeyed to Sorok Island. Sorok Island, which is so named because of its resemblance to a fawn, is an extraordinarily picturesque place. In the park located at its centre many kinds of trees and flowers grow in abundance. After looking around the majestic island, I felt a great pity for those people who have no deep connection to the land. Though the rows of pine trees are inarticulate, they seem to teach us that to be physically handicapped is nothing compared to the spiritual handicap which prevents communion with nature.

What people commonly call travel is not true travel but just an exercise in sight-seeing. Observing is not experiencing. They are rare individuals indeed who have felt the sublimity of nature and learned of the harmonious coexistence of community and nature. We have become content with the tour bus and the guidebook, with a checklist of monuments and with logging all the requisite snapshots; we seldom leave the well-trodden path in order to make our own discoveries. We have forgotten that true travel means strangeness and risk and discovery.

Take a risk this summer and travel away from the beaten path. Undertaking a true journey during summer vacation will give you a landscape in your mind to which you can return throughout your life.

(*Source*: http://www.hongik.ac.kr/~tidings/no_95/09.htm)

Comprehension

1. Why does the author compare travel with narcotic and antidote?
2. Why does the author leave Seoul?
3. What are the disadvantages of low-budget travel?
4. What are the advantages of low-budget travel?
5. Why does the spring move the author?
6. Why does the author feel pity for some people?
7. What do the trees teach us?
8. How does the author differentiate true travel from what people commonly call travel?

Understanding Checklists

A checklist is a list of things that you must remember to do. It aids your memory and ensures that what you need to do is done without any omissions.

Look at the checklist below for sending in your application for higher studies.

	Yes or No Questions	Yes	No
1	Have you filled in all columns?		
2	Have you attached photocopies of all relevant documents?		
3	Have you enclosed the demand draft for registration fee?		
4	Have you pasted your passport size photo in the space provided?		
5	Have you signed in the specified places?		

You may also list points or imperatives beginning with 'check' and prepare your checklist. The example given above will help you to develop a professional approach to preparing checklists.

Choose any two of the following contexts and prepare suitable checklists.

1. Your friend wants to buy a laptop. Help him by preparing a checklist of what to keep in mind when buying a laptop.
2. Your brother has to travel to New Delhi. Give him a checklist for his travel.
3. You are going to travel long distance by car. Help yourself with a checklist so that your journey is trouble-free and comfortable.
4. Your department is organising a function. Give a checklist to the head of your department to ensure the successful conduct of the function.

5.5 Hypersonic Travel

Thinking and Interaction

Discuss the following questions in pairs and share your answers with the class.

1. What is the travel time from Hyderabad to Delhi by train?
2. What is the travel time from Hyderabad to Delhi by flight?
3. How can the air travel time be reduced further?
4. Which is the fastest flying commercial passenger aeroplane in India?
5. Which is the fastest flying military aircraft in the world?

Word Power

Give antonyms for the words in column A by adding a suitable prefix.

	A	B
1	available	
2	possible	
3	personal	
4	expected	
5	integrated	

Reading

Read the passage and answer the questions that follow.

From Hyderabad to New Delhi in 20 minutes flat! Sounds fiction today, doesn't it. But wait, aeronautical engineers are optimistic that it is in the realm of the possible, in the near future. Today, the flying time between the two destinations is 120 minutes by the available commercial aircrafts. Indian defence scientists have firmed up a project that aims to design and build a Mach 6.5–7 speed aircraft that can turn this fiction into fact.

The French Concorde aircraft, which was decommissioned sometime ago reached Mach 2 speeds, which is about 2,000 km/hr. "It is not the speed of travel that matters but the sudden, high-speed acceleration that is required during take-off and the deceleration during landing, wherein all the forces are felt by the passenger," explained Dr Prahlada, Director of the Defence Research and Development Laboratory (DRDL), which is working on such projects.

"For example, a space shuttle travels at very high speeds. Similarly, the man landing on the moon or the recent Chinese manned mission to space, are all good feedback on the familiarisation of space travel at many Mach speeds (faster than the speed of sound)," Dr Prahlada said.

"Not just this, the future aviation scenario would include the development of a personal aircraft like the personal computer, an environment-friendly aircraft run on fuel cells, and a silent aircraft. These challenging technological projects are engaging the attention of aeronautical engineers worldwide. India is among the countries in the fray and positive developments are expected in the next 20–30 years," Dr Prahlada said.

The DRDL has embarked on a project called Hypersonic Technology Demonstrator Vehicle (HSTDV), which will use air-breathing technologies that would lead to development of hypersonic cruise vehicles, which can carry and deliver different payloads at Mach 6.5–7 (many times the speed at which sound travels). "We are hoping to get a clearance from the Central Government for the Rs 250–260 crore project. We will start with the technology demonstrator, including development trials, which would take three years," he said.

"Many developed countries are actively pursuing hypersonic air breathing technologies, which have potential applications in military, space, and civilian areas. They also promise low-cost possibilities and could be 're-usable'," the DRDL chief said.

The HSTDV project aims to demonstrate air-breathing cruise flight at hypersonic speed of Mach 6.5–7, using an airframe integrated scramjet engine, which in turn would use hydrocarbon fuel that is easy to handle. Since the hypersonic cruise vehicles encounter hostile environment, which includes high surface temperature during flight, they need special material that can withstand extreme heat and a thermal protection. Hence, a range of carbon-composites, nickel-based super alloys, niobium alloys and high thermal conducting copper alloy, etc., need to be developed.

A network of experts at the academic institutes, national laboratories, and other Defence Research and Development Organisation labs has already been established to give a thrust to this frontier technology area. 'The network of institutes is expected to chip in with their respective capabilities to put them together,' Dr Prahlada said.

(*Source*: http://www.blonnet.com/2005/01/12/stories/2005011202860300.htm)

Comprehension

1. What have the Indian defence scientists planned?
2. What is the speed of the French Concorde?
3. What is crucial in developing a high speed passenger aircraft?
4. What are the future possibilities in aviation?
5. What technology does HSTDV use?
6. Which fuel is easy to handle?
7. Which special materials are required for hypersonic cruise vehicles?

Understanding Abbreviations

DRDL and DRDO are research organisations in India. What do the following abbreviations stand for? Also mention where these organisations are located.

1. ISRO –
2. CSIR –
3. PRL –
4. TIFR –
5. IISc –
6. CLRI –
7. CCMB –
8. JIPMER –
9. AIIMS –
10. SERC –

Word Power

Read the first two paragraphs of the passage again and find three pairs of antonyms.

1.
2.
3.

Word Formation

Combine the following prefixes and words to form as many words as possible. For example, 'tele-' can be combined with 'graph,' 'phone,' and 'scope' to make telegraph, telephone, and telescope.

	Prefix		Word
1	a-	a.	biotic
2	aero-	b.	chrome
3	anti-	c.	culture
4	mono-	d.	dynamics
5	micro-	e.	graph
6	macro-	f.	human

(Contd...)

7	multi-	g.	meter
8	photo-	h.	phone
9	poly-	i.	plane
10	sub-	j.	scope
11	thermo-	k.	syllabic
12	tele-	l.	theism

Units of Measurement

Understanding the SI units of measurement is essential for technical writers and professionals. They must use the system properly and carefully, according to the internationally accepted conventions.

Look at the following two tables and fill in the blanks.

Table 1

	Physical quantity	**Name of unit**	**Symbol**
1	length		
2	mass		
3	time		
4	electric current		
5	thermodynamic temperature		
6	luminous intensity		
7	amount of substance		

Table 2

	Physical quantity	**Name of unit**	**Symbol**
1	frequency		
2	force		
3	pressure		
4	energy or work		
5	power		
6	electric charge		
7	electric potential		

Bring out the differences between the following.

1. Mach and Decibel
2. Celsius and Fahrenheit
3. Ampere and Coulomb
4. Volt and Power
5. Newton and Pascal

Prepositions

Fill in the blanks with suitable prepositions.

Air travel is a common mode .... travel .... millions. .... the increasing competition .... the airlines, more people are likely to travel. More than one billion people travel .... air each year and .... the majority .... people it is safe. Despite the current security concerns, air travel is likely to remain one .... the best modes .... transport. But it can be a problem .... people .... problems .... the lungs especially .... increase .... the number .... survival years, thanks to the increasing medical research.

.... the introduction .... modern aircrafts, passengers will be exposed .... an altitude .... 8,000 feet and .... some cases exceeding 20 hours. Apart .... the potential .... increasing risks .... medical illness there are lots .... physiological disturbances that can occur or precipitate a problem .... people.

Personal Letter Writing

Imagine that you have the opportunity to join the DRDL team in designing and producing the hypersonic personal aircraft. Write a letter to your father about your interest in joining the project team. In your letter, explain what career prospects you will have in DRDO and how you will help the country achieve a milestone in avionics.

UNIT 6

HUMAN DYNAMICS AND DREAMS

6.1 Sixth Sense

Thinking and Interaction

Discuss the following questions in pairs and share your answers with the class.

1. What is sense?
2. What are the five senses?
3. What is sixth sense?
4. Why do you think that in some animals certain senses are more heightened than in other animals?
5. Do all human beings have sixth sense?
6. How does sixth sense help develop problem-solving skills?

Word Power

Match the words in column A to their meanings in column B.

	A	B
1	mysterious	a. a bet
2	faculties	b. waves of light vibrated in a single direction
3	psychic	c. in a state of rest or movement unless acted upon by an external force
4	wager	d. difficult to explain or understand

(Contd...)

5	creek	e. move suddenly and quickly in the specified direction
6	polarised	f. form opinions without having definite or complete knowledge or evidence
7	dart away	g. excited, persuaded
8	inertial	h. powers of the body or mind
9	speculate	i. a small river or stream
10	incited	j. concerned with events or processes outside physical or natural laws

Reading

Read the passage and answer the questions that follow.

1. In the mysterious borderland just beyond reach of our five senses, there are many remarkable human faculties which are proven, but not yet understood. Scientific research now suggests the possibility of yet-undiscovered internal 'receptors' which are the seat of such sixth senses. Recent research into the organisation of the nervous system and the brain is thrusting close to these psychic hiding places.

2. In 'lower creatures', the familiar senses such as hearing and seeing are often much more keenly developed than in humans. For example, the supersonic whistle that the dog can hear is inaudible to human ears. An owl on the high limb of a tree can see a mouse stirring in the grass at night. But living things often display senses which are not familiar.

3. Every dog lover has a story to tell about a lost pet who found his way home. Dr R. H. Smythe of the Royal College of Veterinary Surgeons described a wager with a group of soldiers at his cottage in Cornwall, England. The soldiers bet him that his Airedale, taken to their base without being able to touch or see the ground, then released in the middle of his teeming camp, could not get back to its master. Dr Smythe's cottage was on a long seven kilometer wide bay with a narrow creek. The dog was rowed across this bay. Placed in a lorry with high sides, he was driven inland ten kilometers to the camp and turned loose. In less than two days, the dog was back home. He had been seen swimming across one kilometer of water

at the narrow part of the bay. He must have gone forty kilometers along one side of the bay to find the crossing place and then thirty-four kilometers back on the other side.

4. No one can demonstrate how such a 'homing instinct' works. But science has been uncovering the physical mechanisms behind some of the equally mysterious faculties which many animals possess. In 1950, for example, German zoologist Karl von Frisch discovered how bees fly a straight course to flowers, even from as far as six kilometers away. The bees use the plane of polarised light, that is, their eyes are able to follow those sun rays which shine in a fixed direction.
5. Fish rarely collide with other fish under water in the dark; they often dart away if a fisherman on the bank so much as takes a step or knocks ashes out of his pipe. The explanation is at hand. On the flanks of many fish are organs which register extremely slight changes in flow of water. These enable the fish to detect a nearby fin, or even sound vibrations from above the surface of the water. Science has found such subtle things as electromagnetism, radar waves, infra-red rays and inertial forces being sensed by animals.
6. According to biologists, human physical nature is one with all life. The human being potentially possesses all the sense of animals, birds, and fish. If nature were able to utilise such forces as radar in the creation of animal senses, then, presumably, these forces were also available in building our own faculties.
7. At present, scientists can only speculate about the mechanism underlying most of our mysterious 'sixth-sense' perception. However, it is suggested that the thalamus may be the seat of ancient sixth senses, smothered in civilised man yet not extinguished. They may occasionally flare brightly in primitive or unsophisticated people, in children, or in adults under great stress. It is certain that these faculties are incited more freely when consciousness—our new brain—does not override their free play.

(*Source*: *Making the Most of Your Life: A Reader's Digest Guide*, pp. 38–39)

Comprehension

1. What does 'mysterious borderland' mean?
2. What is the role of internal receptors?
3. What does the story of Dr Smythe's dog prove?
4. Who explained the flight behaviour of bees?
5. What helps fish not to clash with each other or escape from predators?
7. Why does the author describe sixth sense as 'ancient'?
8. Why does the author relate lack of adequate sixth sense with civilisation and consciousness?

Note-making

Making notes when reading is a very useful study skill. Making notes not only helps you to remember what you have read and go back to it at a later point of time, but also helps organise your thoughts on a subject. Given below is a commonly used format for making notes. Give suitable paragraph titles and make notes for the text you have just read, using the following format.

A. (Title)

1. (Paragraph title)
(Important points:)
a.
b.
c.

2. (Paragraph title)
(Important points:)
a.
b.
(Sub-points:)
i.
ii.

3. (Paragraph title)
(Important points:)
a.
b.

On completing this task, you would have identified the main points and the sub-points of the passage. In your own writing and speech too, you must organise the main points and the sub-points clearly so that you help your readers and listeners understand your writing/speech easily.

Understanding Pronouns: Cohesive devices

Pronouns are words that take the place of nouns. Pronouns function as cohesive devices as they help link sentences together by referring back to nouns. Look at the underlined words in the third paragraph of the passage. These words are pronouns and they stand for other nouns in the text. In speech and writing, pronouns help show relationship within and between sentences.

Identify what the pronouns given below refer to in the third paragraph of the text. They are listed in the order in which they appear in the paragraph.

1. his –
2. his –
3. him –
4. his –
5. their –
6. his –
7. its –
8. he –
9. he –
10. he –

Types of Pronouns

The eight types of pronouns in English have been listed below with examples.

Personal pronouns (examples: *I, we, you, he, she, it, they*) are used in place of names of people, animals or things.

Possessive pronouns (examples: *my, mine, your, his, her, its, their*) are used to refer to ownership.

Interrogative pronouns (examples: *what, when, where, which, who*) are used to ask questions.

Relative pronouns (examples: *that, which, whose, where, when, who*) stand for the noun before them.

Reflexive pronouns (examples: *myself, ourselves, yourself, himself, herself, itself, themselves*) are used when the subject and object are the same person, animal or thing.

Reciprocal pronouns (examples: *each other, one another*) indicate reciprocal relationship.

Indefinite pronouns (examples: *any, none, some, few, several, many, both, anything, nothing*) refer to unspecified nouns.

Demonstrative pronouns (examples: *this, that, these, those*) stand for something that the speaker refers to distinguishing it from other entities.

Dummy It

Look at the last paragraph of the passage where '*it*' appears in two places. This 'it' does not stand for a single noun. It represents the whole clause that follows '*that*'. When the pronoun 'it' is used to refer to a clause or is used as a subject in a sentence, but does not refer to a noun that appears earlier in the text, the 'it' functions as a dummy it. Learning to use pronouns correctly will help you speak and write coherently.

Paragraph Formation

Rearrange the following sentences to form a coherent paragraph.

1. The device is low-priced, easy to install and operate.
2. The treadle pump is a low-cost, foot-operated water lifting device that is ideally suited for small areas of land.
3. It is committed to ensuring prosperity of poor farmers by developing and disseminating low-cost irrigation technologies.
4. It is also gender-friendly as both men and women can easily operate it.
5. It has developed a micro-irrigation technology called treadle pump.
6. International Development Enterprises, India (IDEI) is an Indian non-profit organisation.
7. It is well-suited for areas with abundant ground water.

6.2 Creative Idea Generation

Thinking and Interaction

Discuss the following questions in pairs and share your answers with the class.

1. What is creativity?
2. How do you think you can develop your creativity?
3. Why is it important to generate creative ideas?
4. How did Newton discover the law of gravity?
5. Who are some of the other great men and women whose innovative ideas changed the world?

Word Power

Match the phrasal verbs in column A to their meanings in column B.

	A	B
1	look at	a. to force a lot of things into a small place
2	give up	b. to do something that you do not want to do because you cannot find any other way of achieving something
3	move onto	c. to happen
4	come about	d. to plan, hope or intend to achieve something
5	cram into	e. to stop doing something
6	resort to	f. to remember or imagine someone or something
7	aim at	g. to examine
8	think of	h. to move from one subject to another

Listening

Listen to the short talk titled 'Creative Idea Generation' and answer the following questions. Listen again, if necessary.

Choose the correct answer.

1. What does the passage primarily deal with?
   a. The generation of critical ideas
   b. The production of innovative ideas
   c. The preparation of instructions
   d. The success of creative ideas
2. What role does your subconscious have in creating new ideas?
   a. It is not concerned with your problems
   b. It retains your problem and does nothing else
   c. It delays the generation of a new idea
   d. It works constantly on your problem until you get your new idea
3. Which of the following approaches to creating new ideas is NOT mentioned in the passage?
   a. Sit and think approach
   b. Cramming approach
   c. Sudden flash approach
   d. Methodical approach

4. Why does the author say that creativity is like any other skill?
   a. It can be learnt by practice
   b. It is not different from other skills
   c. It is a very simple skill
   d. It can be acquired without much difficulty
5. What attitude does the author show towards creativity?
   a. Negative
   b. Indifferent
   c. Neutral
   d. Positive
6. What is the consequence of generating more and more creative ideas?
   a. You use various techniques
   b. You become an expert
   c. You turn out to be a carpenter
   d. You forget the techniques

State whether the following statements are true or false.

1. The author talks about a creative idea.
2. There are any number of methods for creating new ideas.
3. You cannot create new ideas, if you are not intelligent.
4. Practice in creating ideas helps you better.

Proposal writing

When you want to do something new, or get funding from agencies or from your own employer for a certain activity or project, you will need to write a powerful and persuasive proposal. The proposal initiates the process and provides information on the issues the project is concerned with and the proposed method or approach for implementing the project. Once the proposal is accepted, your work can start.

Starting a company itself is a project as is sustaining it and selling it out. Every project needs a project proposal and that is why planning the project is such a significant task.

What is a project proposal then and how does one write it successfully? A project is a piece of planned work or an activity which is completed over a period of time and intended to achieve a particular aim. A proposal is a written suggestion. So, a project proposal is a written suggestion for a planned activity to achieve a specific objective.

In the professional context, you may have to write internal or external proposals. In both cases, your proposal must have the following elements.

1. Title page
2. Letter of transmittal
3. Table of contents
4. Executive summary (abstract)
5. Introduction
6. Discussion (main matter)
7. Conclusion
8. Recommendations
9. Glossary
10. References
11. Appendix

The title page will carry the exact title of the project and information on who prepared the proposal for whom, when, and who it is to be approved by.

The letter of transmittal, that is, the cover letter, gives an overall view of the whole project.

The table of contents will give details of the topics covered in the proposal and the corresponding page numbers.

The executive summary should give a gist of the proposal as briefly as possible without omitting the major details. Executives who do not have time to read the whole proposal may look at the abstract to judge the merit of the proposal. Hence, it is extremely important to write a complete but concise abstract. The best abstract will focus on the problem identified, the solution proposed, and the benefits of the proposal to the company, the funding agency or society at large.

The discussion section will be divided under several subheadings and present the relevant details under each heading. Some possible subheads are listed below.

The problem
The available solutions
Proposed solution
Description of material and men
Time schedule
Evaluation mechanism
Budget estimate

The conclusion will summarise the salient features of the proposal, reiterating the benefits for the target group.

The recommendation section will list actions to be taken for successful completion of the work proposed.

The glossary should provide definitions for key terms used in the proposal.

The references section lists the books and documents used for the preparation of the proposal.

The appendix carries any important information which cannot be presented as part of the main text. Usually, some charts and tables find place here.

As a student, you may find it difficult to get a feel of the work place right now, but it is a good idea to think about what kind of work you will be doing in future.

Prepare a short proposal of four to five pages for the following situation. Page limits for each section are listed below.

Letter of transmittal–one page
Executive summary–half a page
Introduction–half a page
Discussion of the main sections–one and a half pages
Conclusion and recommendation–half a page with at least two recommendations

You are working with BSNL as a customer care engineer for cell phones. You receive hundreds of complaints every day about loss of cell phones. You have come up with an innovative idea to locate lost cell phones using a new technology. But you have to do some research, conduct some field work, and prove the usefulness of the idea in order to design a software to detect lost cell phones.

Write a project proposal to the Secretary of the Department of Telecommunications, Government of India (New Delhi–110 002) to support you financially to carry out the project successfully for the benefit of customers.

Insight

If you offer creative and practicable solutions to your company, you will become a valuable employee.

6.3 Pierre and Marie Curie

Thinking and Interaction

Discuss the following questions in pairs and share your answers with the class.

1. How do some people achieve great things in life against all odds?
2. Who are some of the great achievers from our country?
3. What is patenting?
4. Why is a patented product costlier than a non-patented one?
5. When you discover or invent something, will you apply for a patent? Give reasons for your answer.
6. What does IPR stand for?

Word Power

Match the words in column A to their meanings in column B.

	A	B
1	radioactivity	a. lack of the basic things that are necessary for an acceptable standard of living
2	therapeutic	b. rewarded or honoured with a medal
3	customary	c. the quality that some atoms have of producing energy, which can be very harmful to health
4	privations	d. usual activity
5	decorated	e. causing someone to feel happier and more relaxed or healthier

Reading

Read the passage and answer the questions that follow.

And finally Pierre and Marie lured out the secret—two secrets. For instead of one they found two new elements—a substance which they named polonium after Marie's native country, and another substance which they called radium.

The nature of polonium was amazing enough. Its radioactivity was ever so much more powerful than that of uranium. But the nature of radium was the eighth great wonder of the world. Its power of radiation was found to exceed that of uranium by one and a half million per cent.

It was customary for the recipients of the Nobel Prize to call for it in person at Stockholm. But the Curies were unable to make the journey. They were too ill. Quietly, modestly, humbly, they went on with their work—and with their privations. They spent all their money on their further experiments and remained gloriously forgetful of their personal interests. When the therapeutic value of radium was established—it had been found effective, among other things, in the treatment of cancer—their friends urged upon them the necessity of patenting the process of extracting radium. To do so would have meant considerable wealth to the Curies, since radium was valued at $150,000 a gram. But they refused to derive any income from their discovery. "Radium is an instrument of mercy and it belongs to the world," they said.

They refused not only profits but honours as well. All they asked of the world was to give them a good workroom for their experiments. When the Dean of the Sorbonne wrote to Pierre that the minister had proposed his name for the Legion of Honour, Pierre—seconded by Marie—replied as follows: "Please be so kind enough to thank the Minister and to inform him that I do not feel the slightest need of being decorated, but that I am in the greatest need of a laboratory."

(*Source*: *Living Biographies*, Orient BlackSwan)

Comprehension

Choose the correct answer.

1. It can be inferred from the passage that
   a. Scientists need honours to discover new things
   b. Scientists do not need any honours at all
   c. Scientists need encouragement and infrastructure
   d. Scientists have to suffer in life
2. Which of the elements is NOT mentioned in this passage?
   a. Polonium
   b. Uranium
   c. Radium
   d. Thorium
3. The Curies refused to patent the process of extracting radium because
   a. They considered radium as belonging to the world
   b. They did not need any money
   c. They did not want to become rich
   d. They devoted themselves to the cause of science

4. The Curies did not think the French honour important because
   a. They were arrogant
   b. They were sincere
   c. They were neglected by the French
   d. They were more interested in a laboratory
5. The Curies did not go to Stockholm because
   a. They had no money
   b. They were ill
   c. They had no time
   d. They had no friends in Stockholm
6. What is the unique feature of radium?
   a. It got the Curies their Nobel Prize
   b. It was discovered by the Curies
   c. It is expensive
   d. It is effective in the treatment of cancer

State if the following statements are true or false.

1. Both Pierre and Marie Curie were determined to discover two elements.
2. Marie was patriotic.
3. The Curies did not give importance to their personal welfare.
4. The Dean of the Sorbonne was angry with Pierre.

Choose the appropriate definition for the given words or phrases as they are used in the text.

1. lured out
   a. attracted
   b. found
   c. achieved
   d. attempted
2. call for
   a. receive
   b. get
   c. appear
   d. visit
3. urged upon
   a. recommended strongly
   b. requested sincerely

c. convinced without doubt
d. prevailed upon

Pronoun Identification: Cohesive Devices

Identify the pronouns in the first and second paragraphs of the passage, and state their type and what they refer to.

Role Play

Working in groups of four, write a short dialogue for the following situation and enact it.

The Minister of Science and Technology of the Government of France, is entrusted with the responsibility of persuading the Curies to accept the French honour. He visits their laboratory and speaks to them. He also takes the Dean of Sorbonne along with him. He discusses their problems with the dean and assures the Curies that a new research laboratory will be built for them.

6.4 Online Sale of Rabindranath Tagore's Works

Thinking and Interaction

Discuss the following questions in pairs and share your answers with the class.

1. What is art?
2. What is the importance of fine arts?
3. How can technology help in promoting art?
4. Do you know any educational institution established by an artist?
5. Can you name some Indian universities that have been set up to honour artists and writers?

Reading

Read the passage and answer the questions that follow.

1. Rabindranath Tagore's classics, paintings, sculptures, and songs (in compact discs) are soon to be made available for sale at the click of the mouse. Also, on offer through an e-commerce portal, will be the premier publications of Visva-Bharati University, founded by the poet in Santiniketan in 1921. The authorities

are set to launch what they claim "one of most ambitious e-commerce initiatives undertaken by any Central University."

2. The portal developed by a reputed information technology company and hosted at its website, www.braineware-india.com will be linked to the university's official website, visva-bharati.ac.in to facilitate access to the university's wide range of products and publications to national and international buyers.

3. Initially, books published by Visva-Bharati—nearly 700 titles and about 500 titles of Tagore alone—will be available through the online store. Subsequently, the product catalogue, complete with a price list will be upgraded to include Tagore's other works of art like songs, sculptures, and nearly 2000 of his paintings. Finally, to be made available are personalised gift items, specially designed by the university selected from a range of its private collections as well as those gifted to it.
4. They include the Nobel Laureatc's letters, paintings, and cassettes containing records of his voice. Buyers will be able to select products of their choice from the online catalogue and add them to a virtual shopping cart. After checking out, they will be required to make online payments through the payment gateway integrated with the portal that accepts both credit cards and net banking payments.

(*Source*: *The Hindu*, 9.3.2005, p.13)

Comprehension

1. Who established Visva-Bharati University?
2. What is the purpose of making Tagore's works available online?
3. Why is one web address linked to another?
4. What are the different kinds of works by Tagore?
5. How can buyers make payments?

One-word Substitution

Pick out words from the passage that mean the following.

1. The art of making figures, objects, etc., by carving wood or stone, shaping clay, pouring metal into moulds

2. Selling goods on the Internet
3. First in importance
4. One who writes poems
5. Actively seeking success, wealth, status, etc.
6. A place of higher learning for different branches of knowledge
7. Renowned and leading
8. A place on the Internet where you can find information about something, especially a particular organisation
9. To make an action or a process easy
10. A complete list of items, usually in a special order and with a description of each

Understanding Conjunctions

A sentence or a paragraph with a well-knit structure is achieved not only by using pronouns or reference words but also by using conjunctions. Conjunctions are words that conjoin, that is, connect and show the relationship between two words, phrases, clauses, or sentences.

The seven conjunctions which connect two independent clauses are called co-coordinating conjunctions. These are *for, and, nor, but, or, yet,* and *so*. These can be remembered through the acronym FANBOYS.

Listed below are the coordinating conjunctions and their specific functions.

For – reason/purpose
And – addition
Nor – negative choice
But – contrast
Or – positive choice
Yet – concession
So – deciding reason/inference

Read the passage again and underline the sentences that have these connective words. Also, pay close attention to how these words link one sentence with another in the passage.

Fill in the blanks with suitable coordinating conjunctions.

A shy, unassuming scientist .... former civil servant, Rachel Carson seemed an unlikely candidate to become one of the most influential women in modern America. .... Carson had two lifelong passions—a love of nature .... a love of writing—that compelled her in 1962 to publish *Silent Spring,* the book that awakened environmental consciousness in the American public .... led to an unprecedented national effort to safeguard the natural world from chemical destruction.

Connecting Adverbs

Look at the italicised adverbs in the third paragraph: *initially, subsequently,* and *finally*. These adverbs contribute to the cohesion of the passage by indicating different stages in the process of making Tagore's works available for online sale. Connecting adverbs are used to show the relationship between a clause and preceding clause, sentence or paragraph. Some other connecting adverbs are *accordingly, therefore, moreover* and *nevertheless*.

Personal Profiles

Rabindranath Tagore can be described as a poet, writer, painter, singer, lyricist, sculptor, dancer, artist, playwright, educationist, patriot, Nobel laureate, and so on. He wrote poems, short stories, novels, songs, plays, letters, etc. He painted, sculpted, established a university, worked hard for the freedom and welfare of our country, and received the Nobel Prize for literature.

Desribe at least two such multifaceted personalities in a short paragraph each.

Know Yourself

Answer the following questions as accurately and honestly as possible.

1. What are the things that you are good at?
2. Do you have any ambitions?
3. What will help you achieve your goals?
4. What distracts you easily?
5. Why do you have to achieve anything at all?

Insight

> Introspection and self-analysis are valuable tools for all of us to know who we are and to understand what we do. If we understand ourselves, we will stop blaming others and start taking responsibility for all our actions. Only then can we shape our destiny meaningfully.

Paragraph Writing: Self-description

Based on your answers to the above questions, describe yourself in about 125 words.

Food for Thought

"Self-understanding and self-knowledge are the key to breaking the barriers to success."

Formal E-mail Writing: Placing an Order

Write an email to place an order in the following context. Write out your e-mail in the proper format in your notebook.

That the paintings of Rabindranath Tagore are available for sale and you are interested in buying some of them. Send your order to: order@visvabharati.ac.in.

Note: Although the paintings are for your own personal use. The e-mail must maintain some degree of formality. Do not use symbols or short forms of words when placing an order. Be as clear and detailed as possible.

6.5 Continuous Transformation

Thinking and Interaction

Discuss the following questions in pairs and share your answers with the class.

1. Who are some of the top business leaders of India?
2. Who founded Infosys, Satyam and Wipro?
3. How do corporate leaders contribute to the Indian economy?
4. What has continuous learning to do with business and industry?
5. Why do great leaders tell us to dream?

6. Who are some of the world leaders well-known for their inspiring speeches?
7. What helps successful speakers connect with their audiences?

Word Power

Match the words in column A to their meanings in column B.

	A	B
1	exhilarating	a. spreading easily from person to person
2	heroism	b. responses and reactions to an action
3	candid	c. fond of or delighted by something
4	misfortune	d. causing happiness
5	disruption	e. follow something in order to capture it
6	pursue	f. the qualities of courage, boldness, and strength
7	enamoured	g. disturbance to peace or order
8	contagious	h. honest and open about what one thinks
9	mediocrity	i. bad luck
10	feedback	j. fairly low quality

Reading

Read the passage and answer the questions that follow.

Azim Premji's Convocation Address at the Indian Institute of Management at Kolkata, on April 3, 2004

Distinguished Director and faculty of IIM–Calcutta, Guests, and my young friends,

I am very happy to be with you this afternoon. Indian Institute of Management–Calcutta, is one of the earliest management colleges of higher learning to be set up in the country. The pioneering spirit continues even after IIM–C has transformed itself into a world class institution. In your two years here, you must have experienced the enormous change in your own understanding of business and management. Graduation is not the end but the beginning of learning and change. I have found that people who succeed most in their careers are those who can constantly transform themselves. Transformation is not so much a process, as a deep seated desire to change ourselves and our environment. Based on my own experience, I would like to share with you my thoughts on how to make continuous transformation possible. I hope you find them useful.

First, you have got to have a dream. Dreams are very powerful internal motivators. Great achievements are created twice—first in the mind and then in a concrete form.

The most exhilarating part of being young is the ability to dream. As one grows, one may realise that not all of them are achievable. But never turn cynical. Aging is not adding on years. It is parting with one's dreams. Use your experience to reshape your dreams and adapt them to changing reality but do not stop dreaming. I cannot think of a single transformation or achievement, individual or social that did not begin with a dream. Dreams not only help us in seeing things before they happen, but they also give us the passion and energy to make them happen.

Second, stay on course even if you stumble. When everything seems to go wrong, you can either give up or you can let misfortune transform you into something stronger. The difference between great achievement and mediocrity is not extraordinary talent or intelligence, but perseverance. In fact, dreams and perseverance make a winning combination. In 1972, a chartered plane, carrying a Rugby team, crashed in the Andes. After a week long futile search, the rescue team gave up thinking that all of them must be dead. The passengers, after waiting for many days to be rescued, decided to help themselves since apparently nobody else was going to do it. Two of them volunteered to cross the mountains by foot to reach the green valleys of Chile and bring back help. It was a walk of more than fifty miles. But they did it and came back to rescue their fellow passengers who managed to survive in the mountain seventy days after the crash. The core of heroism lies in the ability to walk that extra mile. As long as you can do that, you will never be defeated.

Third, do not be afraid to admit your ignorance. While it is important to project what we are good at, we must be equally candid about areas we do not know enough about. The seeds of learning were sown by the great philosopher Socrates who said, "All I know is that I don't know." Today, knowledge is multiplying at such a rapid rate that it is impossible for anyone to know everything. But if we can develop an index system by which we at least know with whom or where the knowledge is available, we have achieved quite a bit! And there will still be areas which we will be unable to tap. The important thing is not to hide behind a false front. People will respect you for your honesty, if not your wisdom.

Fourth, think about what you will take on next rather than about what you may be letting go. Too many people are so enamoured by the legacy of success in their current roles that they are afraid to look further. This can lead to inertia. If we linger too long on past success, we will miss out on the opportunities that lie ahead of us. We must learn to look at change as an exciting adventure rather than a disruption. New avenues for learning always lie just beyond the shade of our comfort zone.

Fifth, contribute in every situation. The only way to keep learning is by contributing. You do not have to be the leader every time. When a formation of birds flies over long distances, each bird takes its turn in leading. This ensures that no bird gets too tired and yet the formation keeps moving at a certain pace. Every person is important. It doesn't matter whether you play the violin, the flute or the drums; you are still part of the orchestra. Leadership is not about exercising power as much as it is about contributing. This will happen when you realise that leadership is not a privilege but a responsibility.

Sixth, pursue excellence in whatever you do. Excellence cannot be forced through a process nor guaranteed by a certificate. It comes from an all consuming passion to do one's best. It needs an eye for the smallest of details. When differences become small, it is the small things that make the difference.

Seventh, while you must take your career seriously, do not take yourself too seriously. You have to laugh and find humour everyday. This will help you to keep issues in their perspective. Being cheerful is an attitude. Not only will it help you to reduce your own stress, but a positive attitude is contagious. It can do a lot to elevate the moods of people around you and recharge you to take one more shot at the problems facing you.

Eighth, we must always know what we are really good at. Rather than trying to be everything to everyone, we must focus on areas where our talents truly lie. A talent can be defined as that skill which we not only enjoy learning but which we can also learn rapidly. We need to work at honing our talent and smoothening the rough edges. But exceptional performance usually comes from doing what comes naturally to us.

Ninth, always welcome feedback even if it comes in the guise of criticism. I remember the story of a boy who dreamt of becoming an artist but was frustrated because whenever he showed his painting, the teacher would look at it with a frown and find some fault with it. The student improved on his work continuously and he thought he would one day hear a word of appreciation from his teacher. But it never happened. Finally, in disgust, he bought a painting from an accomplished artist, touched it up with fresh paint and showed it to his teacher. To his amazement, the teacher smiled and said, "Now this is really good work. Congratulations." Feeling guilty, the student confessed that it was not really his painting. The teacher looked at him silently and then said, "Till now, I thought you wanted to paint a great picture. But I realise now that you do not want any more corrections, which means that the last painting you did was the best you will ever do. Remember you have set these limits to your talent, not me." Criticism may actually be an expression of faith in us rather than a put down. We must learn to take it constructively because it will show us what more we can learn.

Finally, always play to win. Winning is not about making the other person lose. It is about stretching yourself to your own limits. Once so stretched, you will realise the true extent of your potential. Ultimately, transformation is about reaching and utilising not only your potential but those of others who work with you.

I wish you all the best in your career and in your lives as you step out into a new world.

(*Source*: http://www.azimpremjifoundation.org/html/calspeech.htm)

Comprehension

1. What is the pioneering spirit that Mr Premji talks about?
2. What change does education bring about in college students?
3. What does Mr Premji want to share with the students and the gathering?
4. Why does he say that 'great achievements are created twice'?
5. Does the listing help you understand the speech better? Give reasons for your answer.
6. How does he interpret winning?
7. What do you personally learn from Mr Premji's speech?

Word Power

Find words from the passage for the definitions given below.

1. Continued effort to achieve something one has begun, despite setbacks ....
   ....
2. To imagine something that you would like to happen ....
3. An unusual, exciting or dangerous experience ....
4. Something handed on or left unfinished by a past owner or predecessor ....
   ....
5. An alphabetical arrangement of the main topics, ideas, names, etc. ....
6. A large group of instrumentalists who play together as an ensemble, led by a conductor ....
7. The quality of being extremely good or outstanding ....
8. Objective view of a situation, in which all its elements assume their importance
   ....
9. A way of thinking, behaving and living ....
10. The action or process of indicating the faults of somebody or something ....
    ....

Subordinating Conjunctions

Look at the following sentences.

1. The pioneering spirit continues even after IIM–C has transformed itself into a world class institution.
2. When a formation of birds flies over long distances, each bird takes its turn in leading.

3. While you must take your career seriously, do not take yourself too seriously.

Each of these sentences consists of one independent and one dependent clause. The dependent clause is indicated by words like *after, when,* and *while.* These indicators are known as subordinating conjunctions. They connect a main clause with a dependent clause. These make complex sentences. There are numerous such expressions in English with different meanings and functions. For example, *after* can also be used as a preposition in the sentence: "After a week long search, the rescue team gave up thinking that all of them must be dead." So, you must be careful in learning to use them properly. Your sentence structure may be complex but should convey meanings clearly.

Combine the following pairs of sentences, using suitable subordinating conjunctions. An example is given below.

a. It is important to project what we are good at.
b. We must be equally candid about areas we do not know enough about.

Answer: While it is important to project what we are good at, we must be equally candid about areas we do not know enough about.

Note: The subordinate clause and the main clause are separated by a comma when the subordinate clause appears first.

1. a. Mr Warren Buffet pledged the bulk of his $44 billion fortune to the Bill Gates Foundation.
   b. The world applauded him.
2. a. Mr Warren Buffet turned his personal wealth into something of great value to society.
   b. He resisted the temptation of starting a new foundation in his own name.
3. a. Philanthropic foundations are unable to spend all their money on charity.
   b. They spend 30 per cent of their money on administering the funds.
4. a. You climb the success ladder.
   b. You have to work harder.
5. a. Edison conducted hundreds of experiments.
   b. He invented the light bulb.

Correlative Conjunctions

Look at the following sentences.

1. Dreams *not only* help us in seeing things before they happen, *but* they *also* give us the passion and energy to make them happen.

2. When everything seems to go wrong, you can *either* give up *or* you can let misfortune transform you into something stronger.

The first is a compound sentence. It has the double connective 'not only . . . but also.' The second is a compound-complex sentence. It has the double connective 'either . . . or' These double connectives are called correlative conjunctions. Some correlative conjunctions are listed below.

whether . . . or
either . . . or
neither . . . nor,
not only . . . but also
both . . . and

These are frequently used in our day-to-day communication. Learning to use them correctly will help ensure better communication.

Read the sixth and eighth paragraphs of the passage and identify the sentences that have correlative conjunctions. Do you see any difference in their usage?

Fill in the blanks with suitable correlative conjunctions.

1. .... Ramanujan .... G. B. Hardy contributed to the world of mathematics.
2. Mozart is .... appreciated in Germany .... in other parts of the world.
3. The mystic is .... a fraud .... a god.
4. .... the scientist .... technologist has any solution to the epidemic disease *chikungunya*.
5. .... you go to Delhi .... you go to Dublin, you find people all the same.

Speech Writing

Imagine that you are the chief executive officer of Indosystems, a multinational company with diverse business interests. The principal of an engineering college has requested you to be the chief guest for the convocation. How will you address the staff and students of the college? First prepare an outline of the main ideas of your speech. Then write out your speech in about 300 words. You may divide the speech into five or six paragraphs. Each of your paragraphs may have about 60 to 70 words.

UNIT 7

NATURAL DISASTER MANAGEMENT

7.1 Floods and Cyclones

Thinking and Interaction

Discuss the following questions in pairs and share your answers with the class.

1. What is a disaster?
2. Do we understand natural disasters completely?
3. What does every natural disaster teach us?
4. What are the common preventive measures against natural disasters?

Word Power

List at least ten words related to natural disasters.

1.
2.
3.
4.
5.
6.
7.

8.
9.
10.

Reading

Floods, cyclones, and other natural calamities have become common occurrences, especially in India. Here is a list of basic precautions to be taken, issued by the National Disaster Management Division. Examine the precautions to understand how instructions are written.

1. Listen to radio/TV for the latest weather bulletins and flood warnings. Pass on the information to others.
2. Make a family emergency kit which should include a portable radio/transistor, torch, spare batteries, a first aid box along with essential medicines, ORS, dry food items, drinking water, match boxes, candles, and other essential items.
3. Keep a hurricane lamp, ropes, rubber tubes, umbrellas, and a bamboo stick in your house. These could be useful.
4. Keep your cash, jewellery, valuables, important documents, etc., in a safe place.
5. If there is a flood, move along with your family members and cattle to safe areas like relief camps, evacuation centres, elevated grounds, etc. where you can take shelter.

During floods

1. Don't enter into flood waters; it could be dangerous.
2. Don't allow children to play in or near flood waters.
3. Don't use wet electrical appliances; check them before use.
4. Don't allow water to stagnate near your house. Water stagnation can breed vector/water borne diseases.
5. Stay away from sewerage lines, gutters, drains, culverts, etc.
6. Be careful of snakes; snakebites are common during floods.

7. Stay away from electric poles and fallen power lines to avoid electrocution.
8. Eat freshly cooked and dry food. Always keep your food covered.
9. Use boiled and filtered drinking water.
10. Keep all drains, gutters near your house clean.
11. Use bleaching powder and lime to disinfect the surroundings.

(*Source*: An advertisement in *The Hindu* 23.7.06, p. 7)

Understanding Instructions and Warnings

Instructions

An instruction is a direction for carrying out a task. One gives the instruction and another follows it. It usually takes the form of direct imperative and is in active voice in present tense. An example is, '*Read the instructions carefully*', which is a standard instruction found in user manuals of various products.

Safety Instructions

When the element of safety is involved, the instruction must be followed strictly. Otherwise there may be loss of life and property. For instance, 'Do not touch the power cord with wet hands' is a safety instruction. If this instruction is not followed it may result in an electric shock.

Warnings

Similarly, a warning cautions people about possible danger, death, and destruction. For example, 'Do not walk in this area' written on the wing of an aircraft cautions maintenance engineers not to go there, as walking on this area may cause harm to the wing and to the engineers. Warning signs and instructions usually have red lettering so that they attract people's attention immediately. In most manuals, it is indicated by an exclamation mark set in a triangle.

Writing Instructions and Warnings

1. Prepare a list of five safety instructions for a chemistry laboratory.
2. Write a set of five safety instructions for fire fighters.
3. Draft a list of five warnings for electrical workers.
4. Make a list of five safety instructions for lift users.
5. Issue a set of five precautions against *Chikungunya*.

Compare Instructions

We commonly use lifts in apartments, hospitals, libraries, office buildings, etc. You will notice that both inside and outside the lift, instructions are given to lift users. Look at the instructions in a lift you use frequently and compare them with the ones you have written. Note the differences.

Writing Styles

Here are two sets of instructions from the Chennai Metropolitan Development Authority (CMDA) for flat promoters. Read and discuss them with your neighbour to find out which set is easily readable and comprehensible. Also, identify the elements that increase or decrease the level of comprehensibility and answer the question that follows.

Set A

1. The details of the approved plan should be displayed at the site.
2. The flat should be constructed as per the approved plan.
3. The completion certificate should be obtained from the CMDA after completion of the building.
4. The entire undivided shares of land should be transferred to the flat buyers.
5. The flat buyer should be asked to contact the CMDA for any clarification.

Set B

1. Display the details of the approved plan at the site.
2. Construct the flat as per the approved plan.
3. Transfer the entire undivided shares of land to the buyers.
4. Obtain the completion certificate from the CMDA after completion of the building.
5. Ask the buyers to contact the CMDA for any clarification.

Which set of instructions do you think is clearer? Give reasons for your answer.

Group Discussion

In groups of four or five, discuss why people generally don't like to follow the instructions given below, though these are meant for their safety and welfare. Also, suggest possible ways of helping people understand the need to protect their lives and that of others. Group leaders may then report their group's views to the class.

1. Do not use cell phones while driving.
2. Don't drink and drive.
3. Wear helmet.
4. Avoid rash driving.
5. Obey traffic rules.
6. Do not overtake.
7. Wear seat belt.
8. Keep your cell phones switched off.
9. Do not smoke.
10. Keep the pollution emission from your vehicle under control.

Direct and Indirect Speech

In direct speech the exact words of the speaker are given in quotation marks and in indirect (reported) speech what is said by the speaker is reported without using quotation marks.

Read the following report carefully and make a note of the use of direct and indirect speech. Also identify the reporter's narrative in the passage.

1. More than half of the world's major forests will be lost if global temperatures rise by an average of 3°C or more by the end of the century. The prediction comes from the most comprehensive analysis yet of the potential effects of human-made global warming.
2. Extreme floods, forest fires and droughts will also become more common over the next 200 years as global temperatures rise owing to climate change, according to Marko Scholze of the University of Bristol. Dr Scholze took 52 simulations of the world's climate over the next century, based on 16 different climate models, grouping the results according to varying amounts of global warming they predicted by 2100: less than 2°C on average, 2°C–3°C and more than 3°C. He then used the simulations to work out how the world's plants would be affected over the next few hundred years.
3. Alan O'Neill, science director for the National Centre for Earth Observations said: "Some work in this area has been done before looking at the meteorological forecasts for climate change and feeding those into vegetation models . . . this is a much more comprehensive study." Dr Scholze said the effects of a 2°C category were inevitable. This is the temperature rise that will happen, on average, even if the world immediately stopped emitting greenhouse gases. This scenario predicts

that Europe, Asia, Canada, central America, and Amazonia could lose up to 30 per cent of its forests.

4. A rise of 2°C–3°C will mean less fresh water available in parts of west Africa, central America, southern Europe, and the eastern United States, raising the probability of drought in these areas. In contrast, the tropical parts of Africa and South America will be at greater risk of flooding as trees are lost. Dr Scholze says, "A global temperature rise of more than 3°C will mean even less fresh water. Loss of forest in Amazonia and Europe, Asia, Canada, and central America could reach 60 per cent."
5. Dr Scholze said that his work could help to define the concept of dangerous climate change for policymakers. "Dangerous is very objective. We tried to define a dangerous level and see what the risks are," he said.
6. In his definition, climate change becomes dangerous when an event—such as extreme flooding or heat waves—that only happened once every 100 years becomes one that happens every 10 years.

(*Source*: http://www.heatisonline.org/contentserver/objecthandlers/index.cfm?id=6041&method=full)

Some of what Dr Scholze and Alan O'Neill have said are given in direct speech but their speech is mostly reported. The reporter uses present tense of the reporting verb 'say' and in some others past tense of the reporting verb 'said.' What is the difference between these two forms of the reporting verb?

Change the following into indirect speech.

1. Dr Dameris said, "The ozone hole will stay around for another four to five years. We can't expect it to start to recover until 2010 and then it will take another 40 to 50 years to repair completely."
2. German scientists say, "We do not expect recovery, but a return to stronger ozone depletion and deeper ozone holes the next few years in line with the expected lower solar activity."
3. They say, "We do not believe a sustained reversal of ozone depletion started in the late 1990's. A recovery is only pretended."
4. They said, "The computer correctly predicted levels of ozone from 1960 to 2003."
5. Ann Webb said, "It will take decades for the ozone layer to recover fully because the banned CFC's degrade slowly in the atmosphere."

7.2 Preparing for Earthquakes

Thinking and Interaction

Discuss the following questions in pairs and share your answers with the class.

1. What are the earthquakes that you have heard about?
2. Why is there large scale destruction during earthquakes?
3. What is the study of earth called?
4. What is the study of earthquakes known as?
5. How is the intensity of earthquakes measured?

Word Power

Match the words in column A to their meanings in column B.

	A	B
1	plate	a. careful
2	collide	b. relating to an earthquake
3	onset	c. to cause an activity to happen
4	fault	d. peaceful and calm
5	rupture	e. any of the rigid sections that make up the earth's crust
6	set off	f. the moment at which something unpleasant begins
7	teeter	g. to hit violently
8	seismic	h. a crack in the earth's surface where the rock has divided into two parts
9	prudent	i. to appear to be about to fall while moving or standing
10	serene	j. bursting or cracking

Listening

Listen to a short lecture titled 'Preparing for Earthquakes' and attempt the following exercises.

a. Answer the following questions briefly.
   1. How did the Himalayas originate?
   2. How did the Asian monsoon come about?
   3. How do scientists observe faults?
   4. How is the Himalayas a place of potential disaster?
   5. How can civil engineers help people in facing earthquakes?

b. State whether the following sentences are true or false.
   1. The Tibetan plateau moved up due to a collision between two plates.
   2. The colliding plates are Sumo wrestlers.
   3. Scientists cannot exactly predict when earthquakes will occur.
   4. Earthquakes will occur near plate boundaries only.
   5. Delhi, Mumbai, and Chennai can also be affected by earthquakes anytime.
   6. Awareness alone will save the people from earthquakes completely.

c. Complete the following sentences.
   1. GPS stands for ....
   2. The magnitude of a great earthquake predicted by a geologist in the Himalayas is more than ....
   3. The earthquake in Bhuj occurred on ....
   4. The number of people who died at Bhuj is ....
   5. Major Indian cities are prone to ....

Tense

Fill in the blanks with suitable tense forms of the words given in brackets.

Half of Greenland and vast areas of Antarctica are destined to melt if global warming .... (continue) at the same pace until the end of the century, scientists .... (warn). Their research .... (show) that the loss of so much ice .... (trigger) dramatic rises in sea levels, ultimately swamping low-lying islands and coastal regions and threatening the flood defences of cities such as London.

The last time so much ice .... (lose) from the poles—in a period between ice ages 129,000 years ago—global sea levels .... (rise) by 4 to 6 meters.

Experts .... (believe) many coastal regions .... (suffer) long before sea levels .... (rise) significantly, because even a minor rise .... (make) storm surges more devastating and .... (increase) the risk of flooding.

The warning .... (come) from climate scientists who .... (combine) historical records of Arctic and Antarctic ice melting with advanced computer models capable of predicting future environmental conditions.

Attending and Conducting a Meeting

In your professional life, you will be required to attend a number of meetings. As you assume more responsibility, you will also be assigned the task of conducting meetings.

A meeting is a face-to-face communication context where a group of people meet to discuss an issue or a problem. As a member of the meeting, you will be expected to play an important role in the deliberations.

As a member you have to give your opinions, offer suggestions, evaluate the suggestions given by others without offending them, help clarify a point and ask relevant questions. Indifferent and negative behaviour during meetings will not help the organisation grow. Understanding group dynamics is the key to successful participation in meetings.

Organising meetings requires more complex skills. You have to draw up the agenda in consultation with the members, and finalise a date, time, and venue agreeable to all members. You may have to prepare the minutes of the meeting as well. All this means that you have to keep communicating all the time through phone calls, e-mails, faxes, letters, and in person.

There are specific formats for writing minutes. Listed below is the key information that the minutes should contain and the order in which it must appear.

1. Title of the meeting
2. Day and date of the meeting
3. Venue
4. Members present
5. Members absent
6. Special invitees
7. Points discussed and resolutions adopted
8. Thanks to the chair
9. Signature and name of the chairperson

A sample of the minutes of a meeting has been provided. After a minor earthquake in Chennai, the Chairman of a car manufacturing company has called for a meeting to discuss the damages incurred.

Prosperity Automobile Company
34, Poonamali High Road
Chennai-600 065

MINUTES OF THE 25TH EXECUTIVE BODY EMERGENCY MEETING HELD AT THE SEMINAR HALL ON 25.7.2009 AT 10 AM

The following members were present:

1. Mr Satish Kulkarni, Chairman
2. Mr Piyush Lal, Vice-President
3. Mr Humayun Ahmed, Administrative Officer
4. Mr Pratap Kumar, Security Officer
5. Dr Suresh Gandhi, Seismological Expert (Special Invitee)

The members of the executive body discussed the earthquake that shook Chennai on 24.7.2009 and adopted the following resolutions.

1. Undertake complete assessment of the buildings regarding their ability to withstand earthquakes.
2. Adopt the just-in-time approach for manufacturing and despatching cars from the plant.
3. Tie up with a professional body that will warn against any possible threat of natural calamities for early information and precaution.
4. Insure all company staff and properties against any natural calamity with an international insurance agency.
5. Entrust all works related to safety against natural calamities to the security officer who would work in close association with the Chairman.

The meeting ended with a vote of thanks to the chair.

(Satish Kulkarni)
Chairman

Writing Minutes

Imagine that you are working for a construction company located on the banks of a river. Unprecedented rains have wreaked havoc in your city. Your company premises also suffered damages. You participated in a meeting convened by your chairman. Write the minutes of the meeting convened to discuss the damages and the future course of action.

Recommendation Writing

Read the following passage paying close attention to the language used for writing recommendations.

Introduction

As Chennai is located in a vulnerable part of Peninsular India—the Deccan Plateau—and is flanked by the Bay of Bengal and the Arabian Sea—it is frequently subjected to overwhelming devastation by natural calamities due to cyclonic storms and flooding in its coastal districts. Therefore, our buildings <u>should</u> incorporate disaster resistant features. Besides the very high velocity winds, the coastal areas suffer from the onslaught of seawater over the coast due to storm surge generated by cyclones.

Recommendations for Building Disaster-resistant Structures

Site selection <u>should</u> avoid areas likely to be submerged. <u>It is essential to</u> own a site—at least 500m from the shore and have +5m above Mean Sea Level.

Buildings <u>should</u> be constructed on firm and stiff soil because it will be dangerous to build them on weak soil. Hence, appropriate soil investigation <u>should</u> be carried out to establish the allowable bearing capacity and nature of soil.

Weak soils <u>must</u> be avoided or compacted to improve them so as to qualify them either as firm or stiff. Therefore, a site with sufficient bearing capacity and free-from-the-above-defects <u>should</u> be chosen and its drainage condition improved, so that no water accumulates and saturates the ground, especially close to the footing level.

The lateral load due to wind/tidal surge/tsunami <u>should</u> finally be resisted either by walls lying parallel to the lateral force direction (by shear wall action) or by RC frames to which the panel walls are fixed using appropriate reinforcement such as Seismic Bands at window sill and lintel level. This will avoid collapse due to out-of-plane forces.

Walls <u>need</u> to be reinforced by means of horizontal reinforced concrete bands and vertical reinforcing bars. Horizontal beam at the ground level or plinth level <u>must</u> be provided. <u>It is mandatory to</u> provide them at both the places. Continuous lintel <u>has to</u> be provided for the partition wall also and the height of floor should be less than 3000 mm. Cantilevers <u>are to</u> be well anchored to protect them from earthquake damage.

The materials for doors and windows should be wood or pre-cast concrete. It is desirable to provide reinforced bands or ties around the openings and the window frame should be well anchored in the wall. Wherever corrosion is detected, it must be attended by going for proper rehabilitation, if necessary. Lofts, if provided, should have a proper door and should be kept normally closed. Glass panes provided have to be shatter-resistant. Sticking color film on glass panes will make them shatter resistant.

Certain building types such as earthen houses, random rubble masonry, as well as brickwork in clay mud/mortar, should be ruled out of disaster prone zones and costal zones vulnerable to cyclone and tsunami.

Rich mortars involving cement and lime should be used in fired brick and/or coursed stone masonry. Required steel reinforcement must be introduced in the walls in both directions of the building. Light roofs should be properly anchored.

Most of the losses of life in past earthquakes and cyclones and other disasters have occurred due to the collapse of buildings, constructed in traditional materials like stone, brick, and wood which were not particularly engineered to be earthquake and cyclone resistant. The present state of knowledge about structural safety with respect to survival ought to be adopted, though it involves a small extra expenditure.

(*Source*: http://www.hindu.com/pp/2005/10/15/stories/2005101500080200.htm)

Look at the underlined words in the passage. List them under two categories in the table given below.

Modals	**Verbs and Adjectives**

Use the appropriate modal verbs to write recommendations for any two of the following contexts.

1. Your locality has the perennial problem of water scarcity. List at least ten recommendations for solving this problem.
2. The coastal areas of Orissa and Andhra Pradesh suffer heavy damages every year due to floods and cyclones. Write down ten recommendations for reducing the suffering of people living in these areas due to this problem.
3. Globalisation has opened new avenues for employment, but the students coming out of colleges are found to be wanting in necessary skills. Give a list of ten recommendations to improve the quality of training provided to students in colleges.
4. Creating better infrastructure and providing food, shelter, health, education, and employment in India is the biggest challenge for any government. Write ten recommendations to create these.

7.3 Ride the High Tide

Thinking and Interaction

Discuss the following questions in pairs and share your answers with the class.

1. What is tsunami?
2. How is a tsunami caused?
3. When did the tsunami hit India?
4. Have you read, listened to or watched tsunami experiences?
5. What solutions are available to tackle tsunamis?

Word Power

Match the words in column A to their meanings in column B.

	A	B
1	recount	a. representing or describing something or somebody
2	calamity	b. a very sad event, situation, involving death, destruction or suffering
3	the deep	c. to describe how something happened
4	portrayal	d. the force that some people think controls what happens and which cannot be influenced by people

(Contd...)

5	tragedy	e. a serious accident causing damage
6	destiny	f. the sea

Reading

Here is a review of a book on tsunami for children. Read through it, noting the structure and organisation of a book review.

My Friend, the Sea is the story of a boy who recounts life the way it was before calamity struck on December 26, 2004. The boy also talks of his missing father and friends, while hoping to start life anew. Photographs of the sea and the narrative try to bring out the essence of life by the deep.

The book is a positive portrayal of emotions that come alive after tragedy. The story is a first person account by a boy, who is puzzled over the sudden changes in his life and, though troubled, hopes for a new tomorrow.

The book flows from an earlier version *Suresh and the Sea,* which was part of a series that explored the relationship between man and his environment. Suresh is from the fishing community, and is happy about his destiny. "My mother's cooking never tastes as good as when we eat it in the middle of the sea," he says, in contrast to what the boy in *My Friend, the Sea* feels. "I miss my mother's cooking," says the boy looking at his mother lost in thought. Her husband is missing.

"Toys and books in English were given to children affected by the tsunami. But, there were no books in Tamil. Students from a small city called Pegau in Germany funded the publishing of a book in Tamil, which voluntary groups working with tsunami-affected children can use. They raised 1000 Euros and helped us bring out *Kadalum Naanum,*" said Radhika Menon, Director, Tulika, about the Tamil version of the book. Translated by Shubashree, "the book uses colloquial language permissible in teaching".

The message is clear. Those deeply affected by natural calamities do not linger over these issues. They believe in moving forward, like the boy in the book.

(*Source*: http://www.hindu.com/yw/2005/05/20/stories/2005052000780800.htm)

Comprehension

1. How does the review begin?
2. How does the author summarise the whole book in two sentences in the second paragraph?

3. Why does the author relate this book to a series of books?
4. Why does the author mention the funding from Germany?
5. How does the review end?

Word Origin: Japanese

Tsunami is a well-known word from the Japanese language. *Samurai, haiku, sudoku, zen,* and *kaizen* are examples of Japanese words commonly used in English. Learn to use these words in sentences of your own and think of some more examples.

Writing Book Reviews

Prepare a review of a book you have read recently and submit this assignment to your teacher. Some of the best reviews may be read out in the class.

7.4 Half of Forest Area Fire-prone

Thinking and Interaction

Discuss the following questions in pairs and share your answers with the class.

1. Why is fire important to us?
2. How is fire a source of danger?
3. Where do huge fire accidents usually occur?
4. What is the environmental impact of such fires?
5. Which international organisations aim at protecting the environment?

Word Power

Match the words in column A to their meanings in column B.

	A	B
1	prone	a. to please and calm someone who is annoyed with you
2	scanty	b. the part of a finished cigarette, bidi, etc. that has not been smoked
3	sporadic	c. soft and not woody
4	herbaceous	d. smaller in size or amount than is considered necessary

(Contd...)

5	propitiate	e. tending to show a negative characteristic
6	advent	f. happening irregularly
7	butt	g. the arrival of an event

Reading

Read the passage and answer the questions that follow.

Altogether, 1.45 million hectares of forests—half the forest area of the country—is fire-prone causing a financial loss of Rs 4,400 millions annually. Almost all forest fires are, intentionally or unintentionally, man-made.

A report, 'Forest Fires in India', brought out by the World Wide Fund for Nature—India, suggests that fifty per cent of the forest area in the country is fire-prone—ranging from thirty three per cent in some States to ninety per cent in others—and about six per cent is prone to major fires.

Ecologists believe that India being located in the sub-tropical region, organic matter decomposition is inherently fast and forest fires may hasten further turning over of the organic matter. This may lead to nutrient loss from the forests and consequently to their large-scale degradation, the report points out.

Comprehensive scientific information on forest fires in the country is scanty and detailed studies are required for better management of forests through fires as in the developed countries where fire is being used as a management tool, the report suggests. 'In India, nothing could be prescribed on the basis of sporadic and location-specific scientific studies. Until comprehensive studies are carried out, control on man-made recurrent wildfires involving local communities seems to be the best strategy', it recommends.

Communities intentionally set fire to forests for various reasons in different parts of the country. The pine (*Pinus roxburghi*) forests are set on fire during summer to promote growth of herbaceous vegetation for fodder during monsoon; forest patches are burnt to practise 'jhum' or shifting agriculture, and fire is caused by the local communities to collect non-timber forest products such as 'Mahua' (*Madhuca latifolia*) fruits or is traditionally set on fire by some tribal communities to propitiate local deities.

In the western side, tribals burn forests to celebrate the birth of a son, and in the Western Ghats, fires are set in the forests on the upper hill slopes just before the advent of the monsoon to use mineral-rich ash that is washed down to make agriculture fields fertile.

In addition, cattle grazers, schoolboys, forest contractors, and forest personnel set fire to forests for various reasons. Sometimes, an individual or a community also sets ablaze forests to take revenge against rivals for one reason or the other.

Among the many causes of accidental fires, the important ones are fire caused due to burning of crop remains from agriculture fields, fire occurring from fire lines during controlled-burning by the Forest Department, a live cigarette or bidi butt carelessly thrown by passersby, vehicle repairs on roads or campfires set up by tourists.

The aim of the pilot study was to gain first hand information from different states, and based on the experience and the lessons learnt, step up the study to highlight the forest fire issue and to facilitate development and implementation of a meaningful national action plan for the control and management of forest fires in the country.

(*Source*: http://www.hinduonnet.com/2003/07/16/stories/2003071605321200.htm)

Comprehension

1. Why are forest fires a serious problem in India?
2. What do ecologists fear?
3. What are the problems with forest fire management in India?
4. Why do some communities set fire to forests?
5. Why do tribal people burn forests?
6. What are the causes of accidental fires?
7. What was the aim of the pilot study?

Understanding Compound Adjectives

Look at the following compound words: *fire-prone*, *man-made*, *large-scale*, *location-specific*, and *mineral-rich*. These are called compound adjectives as they qualify nouns like *area*, *fire*, *degradation*, *studies*, and *ash*. Check the contexts of these compound nouns and see how they are used in sentences. Look at the table below for examples.

	Structure	Examples
1	noun + adjective	fire-prone, accident-prone
2	noun + past participle	man-made, tsunami-affected
3	noun + present participle	path-breaking, problem-solving
4	adjective + past participle	ready-made, quick-witted
5	adverb + adjective	fully-automatic

Explain the following compound adjectives.

1. light-absorbing material
2. state-owned enterprise
3. decision-making process
4. ladder-mounted vehicle
5. locally-available resource

Make compound adjectives from the following phrases.

1. an equipment which fights fire
2. a machine which vends tickets
3. a room which is air-conditioned
4. a diode that emits light
5. an economy which is driven by the market

Look at the following pair of compound adjectives.

a. missile-guiding system
b. missile-guided system

Even though they look similar, they have different meanings. In the first case, the system guides the missile and in the second case, the missile guides the system.

Differentiate the following pairs of compound adjectives.

1. a. satellite-tracking computer
   b. satellite-tracked computer
2. a. wheel-aligning machine
   b. wheel-aligned machine
3. a. algorithm-writing software
   b. algorithm-written software
4. a. product-advertising agency
   b. product-advertised agency
5. a. industry-supporting program
   b. industry-supported program

Writing a Report

To write a good report, you need to collect necessary information from the site, the people involved and from other private or government documents. After collecting the relevant data, it must be analysed so that you can find patterns or reasons for certain actions happening or not happening, and organise your ideas in an easily readable form. You may use graphs, charts, tables, etc., to present your ideas attractively and effectively. At the end of the report, you give your suggestions and recommendations for the possible course of future action. You have to prepare reports as objectively as possible so that sound decisions are taken.

The reading passage is a newspaper report. Analyse the structure of the report and see how various elements are differently placed. For example the aim, which is usually stated at the beginning of a report, is given at the end. Think about the reason for this. Find out other such elements and discuss their placement.

1. *Write a report on a fire accident in an apartment complex where twenty families and two IT service companies are housed.*

2. *Prepare a report on a road accident in which a bus rammed into a car and killed five people on the spot.*

3. *Draft a report on a burglary in the house of an old lady living alone in a suburban area.*

4. *Write a report on an airplane crash on the outskirts of an airport.*

7.5 World Institute for Disaster Risk Management

Thinking and Interaction

Discuss the following questions in pairs and share your answers with the class.

1. What is disaster management?
2. Which are the special institutes/centres/departments for disaster management in India?
3. Why is disaster management given top priority today by world governments?
4. How does nature prove its supremacy over man?

Word Power

Match the words in column A to their meanings in column B.

	A	B
1	dissemination	a. to gather or organise things or people to achieve a particular aim
2	initiative	b. spreading or giving news, information, ideas, etc.

(Contd...)

3	marshal	c. making something less harmful, unpleasant or bad
4	vulnerable	d. a new action or movement to solve a problem
5	anticipate	e. make something happen suddenly or sooner than expected
6	mitigation	f. able to be easily attacked
7	precipitate	g. to imagine or expect something will happen

Reading

Read the passage and answer the questions that follow.

World Institute for Disaster Risk Management (WIDRM) is a network for applied research, implementation, and dissemination in the field of disaster risk management. It is an initiative of the Board of the Swiss Federal Institutes of Technology and Virginia Polytechnic Institute and State University in conjunction with the ProVention Consortium of the World Bank.

Every managing executive in the public or private sector has a duty to ensure appropriate risk management in his area of responsibility. Hazardous events of natural or technological origin can happen anywhere and at any time. It's never too early to integrate risk management into corporate governance—but it may often be too late.

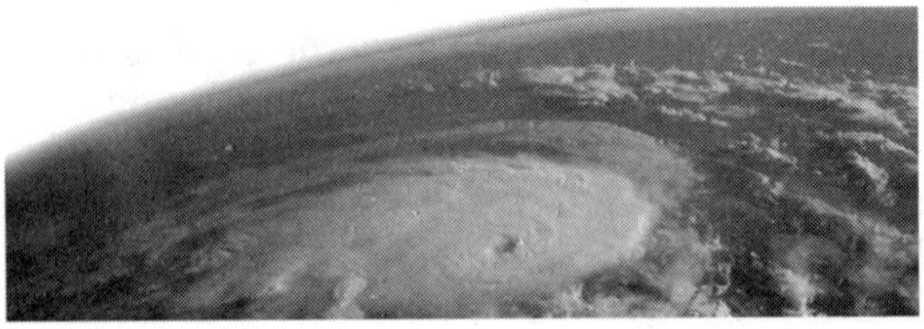

WIDRM marshals resources for collaborative activities in applied research, research applications, and professional practice to reduce disaster risks in vulnerable communities throughout the world.

The objective of WIDRM is to enable people to anticipate disasters and take action to protect life and property, and to ensure sustainable social and economic development. Its activities include supporting the pursuit of an optimal balance between disaster risk reduction, risk-sharing mechanisms, and management of residual risks in the face of limited resources.

WIDRM achieves its aims by filling knowledge gaps, providing a clearing-house for information, building know-how, mobilising resources, and forging partnerships with governments, private enterprises, international agencies, and NGOs.

WIDRM works with a wide range of international organisations and institutions whose common objective is disaster risk reduction for public safety and sustainable development.

Even when reliable and cost-effective technologies are available for early warning, disaster prevention, and mitigation, many governments, especially in developing countries, lack an adequate institutional framework in which to apply them.

Natural and technological disasters often cause substantial damage to life and property, infrastructure, cultural heritage, and the ecological basis of life. Indirect losses in terms of business interruption, loss of production, and loss of services often exceed losses due to direct physical damage. Developing countries are affected more severely, often suffering a dramatic decline in Gross National Product (GNP).

Disaster losses have increased dramatically over the past two decades. This has resulted from changes in the pattern of hazard occurrence and from increased vulnerability of a growing population. With greater pressure to exploit marginal lands and accommodate more people in urban areas, the potential for future disasters continues to expand.

To develop effective and efficient tools and strategies for disaster risk assessment and risk reduction, it is necessary to understand the factors contributing to those risks. Natural hazard events often precipitate subsequent technological failures, and dependency on tightly coupled technological systems can increase the potential for catastrophic failure and disaster. Natural and technological disasters also threaten the ecological basis of life through long-term environmental damage.

(*Source*: http://www.drmonline.net/about/index.htm)

Comprehension

1. Who established the World Institute for Disaster Risk Management (WIDRM)?
2. What are the two sources of hazardous events?
3. Why was WIDRM set up?
4. How does WIDRM achieve its objectives?
5. What problems do developing countries have?
6. What damages are caused by natural disasters?
7. Why are developing countries affected severely?
8. How are natural disasters and technologies interrelated?

State whether the following statements are true or false.

1. Managers in all areas have a great responsibility to deal with natural and technological disasters effectively.
2. WIDRM alone can reduce risks in potential areas.
3. WIDRM is an independent organisation without any relation to other organisations.
4. Indirect losses are heavier than direct losses.

Writing Organisational Profiles

This passage describes the World Institute for Disaster Risk Management (WIDRM) focussing on the following.

- What is it?
- Who established it?
- What relevance does it have today?
- What resources does it gather?
- What does it aim to achieve?
- How does it achieve its aims?
- Who are the partners?
- How is it important for developing countries?
- What is its significance for the environment?

First, collect enough data about the organisation you want to write on. After collecting the data, organise the details with focus on the reader in your mind. For example, if you are writing about a college or university, check its prospectus wherein you find a lot of information about the institution. The prospectus is meant for prospective students to help them choose or decide which college is the best suited for them or recommend it to others.

Similarly, companies that come to colleges for placements also give out company profiles in the form of brochures or leaflets. They prepare such profiles to attract young talent to join them and work for them. In your professional life, you will be expected to write such profiles for many different audiences. Audience awareness, thus, is very important in all writing.

Choose a well-known organisation, institute, centre or department and describe it along the lines of the write-up on WIDRM.

Describe your own college or specifically your department in about three paragraphs of about 100 words each.

Writing Profiles for the Web

You may also have to write a profile of your organisation for the web. Here is an example for a web profile of Anna University, Chennai.

Anna University, Chennai

Anna University, Chennai was established on 4th September 1978 as a unitary type of University. In December 2001, it became a large, highly renowned affiliated University, having brought into its fold about 225 Self-financing Engineering Colleges, six Government Colleges and three Government-aided Engineering colleges located in various parts of Tamil Nadu State. It offers higher education in Engineering, Technology and allied Sciences relevant to the current and projected needs of the society. Besides promoting research and disseminating knowledge gained therefrom, it fosters cooperation between the academic and industrial communities.

(*Source*: www.annauniv.edu)

Go to the websites of reputed companies like Ashok Leyland, Infosys, Philips, General Electric, etc. Collect their profiles and compare the way in which their profiles have been written. You should visit a minimum of two websites for your comparative evaluation of the profiles. Enclose the printouts of the original web profiles along with your assignment.

UNIT 8

QUALITY OF LIFE

8.1 Standards in Daily Life

Thinking and Interaction

Discuss the following questions in pairs and share your answers with the class.

1. What is ISI?
2. Where do you see ISI marks?
3. Why does the government alert people to buying products with ISI marks?
4. How does an ISI-marked product differ from other products?
5. What are some other quality assurance symbols that you see on products and services around you?

Word Power

Match the words in column A to their meanings in column B.

	A	B
1	twilight	a. careful watching of a person or place, especially by police, army, etc.
2	gigantic	b. bringing together different pieces of information to analyse similarities and differences
3	memorandum	c. the act of marking units on a measuring instrument
4	multifarious	d. extremely large
5	statutory	e. a detailed description of something

(Contd...)

6	intrinsic	f. the final part of a period of time
7	criterion	g. of many different types
8	compatibility	h. an informal legal agreement
9	collating	i. important and basic characteristic of something
10	specification	j. controlled by law
11	surveillance	k. being able to exist or work successfully with someone or something
12	calibration	l. a standard by which something is judged

Reading

Read the passage below and answer the questions that follow.

In the twilight years of the British rule in India, when the country was faced with the gigantic task of laying the industrial infrastructure, it was the Institution of Engineers (India), which prepared the first draft of the constitution of an institution which could take up the task of formulation of national standards. This led to the Department of Industries and Supplies issuing a memorandum on 3 September 1946, formally announcing the setting up of an organisation called the Indian Standards Institution (ISI). It was on 6 January 1947 that the ISI came into being and in June 1947, Dr Lal C. Verman took over as its first director. Symbolic of the role, the Indian Standards Institution (ISI) was to play, the first standard drawn was for the national flag of India.

Considerable progress has since been made by the Indian Standards Institution with its multifarious activities like standards formulation, certification, testing of products, international cooperation, and standards promotion. However, a need was felt to provide recognition and status to the organisation to enable it to discharge its functions effectively. Thus the government enacted the Bureau of Indian Standards Act, 1986, which led to the establishment of the Bureau of Indian Standards as a statutory body on 1 April 1987.

Standardisation is intrinsic to life, and we see its many manifestations in nature and life around us. It encourages improvement in the quality of life and makes major contributions to safety, public health, and environment protection.

Standardisation is based on the experiences of daily life. It is the result of a cooperative effort, and is revised from time to time to keep in step with technological progress.

It provides us with a criterion for judgment, a measurement of quality, and a certain guarantee of compatibility and interchangeability.

In the Bureau of Indian Standards (BIS), similar to standards bodies the world over, standards are formulated through technical committees which have representatives from the manufacturers, technical experts, and users. The standards are documents of consensus, which are finalised after taking the views of all those who may have an interest in it.

BIS plays the key role of holding the secretariat for the technical committees and collating and analysing the data and other information which may be required for formulating the standards. It has formulated nearly 17,000 standards which may be categorised as basic standards, product specifications, and methods of test and codes of practices.

With the objective of satisfying the consumer in terms of product quality, the BIS has undertaken various quality certification activities. The domestic consumer is familiar with the ISI mark on a product which is an assurance that the product conforms to the requirements as laid down in the specification. Conformity to the standard is ensured through regular surveillance of the manufacturing process, surprise inspections and testing of samples drawn from the factory as well as from the market. Fraudulent and unauthorised use of the ISI mark is a violation of the law punishable under the BIS Act.

The BIS has established a chain of laboratories at different centres in the country for testing the conformity of certified products and also samples offered by applicants for the grant of ISI marks. These labs also offer specialised services of calibration of test equipment and instruments and procurement of standard reference materials. They also undertake research and development for evolving speedy and effective test methods.

(*Source*: http://pib.nic.in/feature/fe1099/f0810991.html)

Comprehension

1. Who prepared the first draft of the constitution of the ISI?
2. When was the ISI set up?
3. What was the first standard drawn by the ISI?
4. What are the various functions of the ISI?
5. Why was the BIS 1986 Act passed?
6. What role do the technical committees play in formulating standards?
7. How are standards classified?
8. What does an ISI mark mean to the customer?
9. How are standards constantly maintained?
10. What are the functions of the laboratories set up by the BIS?

Understanding Relative Pronouns

Look at the following words underlined in the first paragraph of the passage: *when*, *which*, and *that*. These are relative pronouns. Relative pronouns link one clause to another clause and stand in place of a noun. Relative pronouns help form a complex sentence from two simple sentences. Look at the sentences given below.

It was the Institution of Engineers.

It prepared the first draft of the constitution.

The first '*it*' is called the 'dummy it' whereas the second '*it*' is a personal pronoun. Look at the following sentence to see how these two sentences are combined to form one complex sentence by replacing '*it*' with '*that*'.

It was the Institution of Engineers which prepared the first draft of the constitution.

The above sentence can be rewritten as a simple sentence as follows.

The Institution of Engineers prepared the first draft of the constitution.

The revised sentence tells us who prepared the draft but the first complex sentence, beginning with '*it*' emphasises that it was the Institution of Engineers (and not anyone else) who prepared the draft.

Combine the following pairs of sentences using a suitable relative pronoun.

1. a. It was Dalton.
   b. He said that atoms could not be split.
2. a. It is London.
   b. It is the capital of England.
3. a. It is Harvard University.
   b. It is the world's number one university.
4. a. It is the ISI.
   b. It formulates standards for goods and services in India.
5. a. Mr Prasad is a quality control engineer.
   b. He certifies export worthiness of the products from his company.

Rewrite the following complex sentences into simple sentences.

1. It is the electronic circuit which should be checked first.
2. It was the doctor who administered the medicine to the patient.
3. It is the architect who designs huge buildings.
4. It is the educational institution which should provide for campus placement facility.
5. It is an innovative idea which catches the attention of people.

Rewrite the following simple sentences as complex sentences.

1. William Harvey discovered the circulation of blood.
2. The general theory of relativity was postulated by Einstein.
3. Oxygen and water sustain life on the earth.
4. Carbon monoxide and other harmful substances cause ozone depletion.
5. The manufacturing units must maintain standards in their products.

Writing Memos

Memo or memorandum, is a short written document that is circulated within an organisation. It may be used to exchange information between departments, make recommendations, issue notices, remind someone to do something, give a report on an action taken, etc.

Essentially, a memo has five elements. It must carry details of the recipient and sender, followed by the subject, date and content. If it is of a serious nature, it may contain the name and signature of the sender. These elements may be organised differently in different firms. Usually, the memo is short—not more than a page and rarely two pages long. Given below is a sample in a commonly used format.

To: M. Nagarajan, AO
From: Ravi Varma, PRO
Subject: Repair of photocopying machine
Date: 16.6.2008

The photocopying machine in our department requires the attention of the service engineer. It crackles when copies are being made and the quality of copies is very poor. Sometimes, paper gets stuck in the machine, causing inconvenience.

The service engineer from the company that supplied the machine in December 2006, needs to be contacted. Please help us rectify the problem by 5 p.m. tomorrow.

RV

As you can see from the sample, the problem and the background to it must be clearly stated. The solution or action to be taken must also be stated clearly.

Prepare memos for the following contexts.

1. You are the Chief Manager of a large bank. You faced a serious problem with regard to power supply on a particular day when salaries of thousands of employees had to be processed for that month. You approached the electrical engineer of your branch and he/she did a remarkable job of restoring power supply in just 15 minutes. Write a memo to the electrical engineer appreciating the efforts taken by him/her to restore power supply in such a short time.
2. You are the Human Resources Manager of a big financial services company. You find that a new method of providing financial solutions to corporate companies is going to be discussed in an international seminar in Bangalore. Write a memo to the Chief Executive Officer of your company requesting him for permission to send Mr P. Chandrasekhar of your finance department to attend the seminar.

8.2 Total Quality Management

Thinking and Interaction

Discuss the following questions in pairs and share your answers with the class.

1. What is quality?
2. What is quality management?
3. What is Total Quality Management (TQM)?
4. Do you know some organisations which implement TQM regularly?
5. How is TQM achieved?
6. Would you like to work for a TQM company? Give reasons for your answer.

Listening

Listen to short talk on Total Quality Management and answer the following questions.

1. Which country gave TQM to the world?
2. Why does a TQM company give the highest priority to customer satisfaction?
3. How does TQM ensure quality as a way of life?
4. How does TQM maintain high levels of customer satisfaction?
5. How is quick action helpful to a company?

6. What are the advantages of recognising problems as system-related?
7. How does a TQM company achieve active employee participation?
8. What are the two awards given to companies for quality achievement?

Give two antonyms for each of the words, one with a negative prefix and the other without it. An example has been provided.

	Word	Antonym with negative prefix	Antonym without negative prefix
1	order	disorder	chaos
2	known		
3	important		
4	continuous		
5	satisfaction		
6	functional		
7	consistent		
8	legitimate		
9	directly		
10	divided		
11	rational		
12	appropriate		
13	conformity		
14	successful		
15	communicate		

8.3 Euro vs Bharat Stage Norms

Thinking and Interaction

Discuss the following questions in pairs and share your answers with the class.

1. What are Euro–IV and Bharat Stage III?
2. Where do you often see Euro–IV and Bharat Stage III signs?
3. Who designed and implemented these norms?
4. How do we benefit from these?

Word Power

Match the words in column A to their meanings in column B.

	A	B
1	emission	a. severity, strictness
2	substantial	b. gas, light, heat, etc., that is sent out
3	efficacy	c. new
4	simulated	d. large
5	replicate	e. acting according to a set of rules
6	stringency	f. made to look and feel real
7	compliance	g. ability to produce the intended result
8	innovative	h. to make copies
9	mandate	i. without any order
10	willy-nilly	j. official permission to do something

Reading

Read the passage below and answer the questions that follow.

Euro–III is nearly equivalent to Bharat Stage III, which is the vehicular emission standard proposed by the union government and to be effective from April 2005 in identified metropolitan cities having substantial vehicle population.

This recommendation is based on the Mashelkar Committee report for the auto-fuel policy launched in the country for improvement of air quality. In 2010, Bharat Stage IV equivalent to Euro–IV is envisaged. These norms are introduced such that the changeover is gradual and smooth—first in metros and after a gap of specified time, extended to vehicles plying all over India.

It seems appropriate at the outset, to take a close look at these graduating vehicles and assess their efficacy technologically in controlling air quality standards of our nation.

Transition to Bharat norms

Prescribed Emission Limits		
	CO (g/km)	(HC+NOx) g/km
BS I	2.72/3.16*	0.97/1.30*
BS II	2.20	0.50
	—	HC NOx
BS III	2.30	0.20 0.15
BS IV	1.00	0.10 0.08

The harmful emissions, which are identified for regulations in different Bharat Stages (BS), are carbon monoxide (CO), unburnt hydrocarbons (HC) and nitrogen oxides (NOx). The table gives the prescribed upper limits. Note that HC and NOx are separately controlled in BS–III, while they are bracketed in BS–I and II.

Emission limits for passenger cars are expressed as mass emissions grams per km (g/km) of simulated vehicle drive. The emphasis here is on simulation of actual driving versus assumed driving pattern in a cycle based on long observation and trials on road. In simulation, the vehicle is "exercised" on a "tread mill" called chassis dynamometer, replicating the assumed driving-pattern of the country. This is called the driving cycle of the country. The emissions are measured over the cycle and the results computed to give mass emissions.

In European countries, the regulatory standards are called Euro norms—designated by the letters EU suffixed by numerals I, II, III, and IV in the increasing order of stringency. Although the norms for vehicles vary from country to country reflecting the differences in traffic density and regulation, road infrastructure, fuel quality, maintenance standards, India uses Euro standards with only one modification—lower maximum speed of 90 km/h in the last part of the cycle instead of 120 km/h as mandated in the EU norms. This cycle is called modified European cycle.

The other components of the driving cycle such as idling period, acceleration and deceleration rate periods, and cruising period are exactly the same as Euro practice. The norms derived from this cycle are called Bharat Stage standards—designated by the symbol BS, suffixed by numerals I, II, III, and IV in the increasing order of stringency.

According to the table, the main requirements for BS–III graduation are lower HC and NOx levels, which are now mandated separately. Probably, these are controlled by a higher and/or different catalyst formulation (to oxidise HC in the exhaust) and selected dosage of exhaust gas recirculation (preventing excessive formation of NOx). Naturally, the customers have to meet this extra cost.

The low emission level in BS–III norms is only a necessary, but not a sufficient, condition. For complete equivalence, some more provisions need to be made. One such provision is the on-board diagnostic system (OBD) that can indicate malfunctioning of emission control and engine performance. With this and other specified add-on systems, complete graduation to Euro–III level can be attained.

Efficacy of graduation to Bharat norms

This progress in technology has certainly established India's capability in developing cleaner vehicles and components. Using standards equivalent to the Euro levels certainly encourages export of Indian products.

Such components as catalytic converters, electronic fuel injection devices and design capability for developing cleaner combustion chambers should soon attract the attention of private research and development centres and institutions for more collaborative efforts.

The necessary component required for upgradation to the emission norms is a three-way catalytic converter (TWC) to destroy all the three emissions (HC, CO, and NOx) in a single step. This has close correspondence to an electronic fuel injection (EFI) system through a "Lamda" or oxygen sensor in the exhaust with a feedback to correct the air-fuel ratio for complete destruction of the emissions.

Very little experimental evidence is there to show how fast this acts in the "stop-and-go" driving pattern of India. Yet, Euro-norm compliance requires this expensive item in EFI systems since the carburettor is replaced as per BS–II norms. Most of these devices and sensors are imported. Our equipment manufacturers may have to get them tested elsewhere if facilities are not available at the authorised testing centers.

India must urgently use innovative methods to arrive at mass emissions under actual service conditions. The Society of Automotive Engineers (SAE) literature gives many such methods, some of them from Indian students. After rationalising these methods, we may arrive at appropriate norms in a way equivalent to the Euro norms.

The ultimate aim is that mass emissions into the atmosphere must not exceed the values recommended by international standards. For export purposes however we have to comply with Euro or any other norms acceptable in the foreign market. We have to balance the market forces and the social objective of keeping our air cleaner.

(*Source*: www.thehindubusinessline.com/2005/02/07/stories/2005020700280900.htm)

Comprehension

1. When was BS–III implemented?
2. When will BS–IV be introduced?
3. What are the harmful emissions?
4. What is the major difference between BS and EU standards?
5. What is the function of the On-Board Diagnostic System (OBD)?
6. Why are three-way catalytic converter and electronic fuel injection compared?
7. Why does the author say that India must urgently use innovative methods to arrive at mass emissions under actual service conditions?

Role Play

Imagine that you are the chairperson of the Pollution Control Board of India. A journalist wants to interview you on the steps you have taken to control pollution. Write a brief dialogue between the two. Two students may play these roles in the class.

Paragraph Writing

In a paragraph of about 125 words, compare pollution from state-owned vehicles with that from privately-owned vehicles.

8.4 World University Rankings

Thinking and Interaction

Discuss the following questions in pairs and share your answers with the class.

1. Do you know how universities are ranked globally?
2. Which is the best university in the world?
3. Which is the best university in India?
4. Why do you think very few Indian universities rank among the best in the world?
5. What should we do to develop our universities into top institutions of higher education?

Word Power

Match the words in column A to their meanings in column B.

	A	B
1	credence	a. forming the total of something
2	showings	b. a real or imaginary dividing line
3	exceedingly	c. acceptance or belief that something is true
4	put-up	d. forced something out of its original position
5	devised	e. extremely
6	displaced	f. put together
7	accounting for	g. the quality of someone's performance in a competitive activity
8	axis	h. showed

Reading

Read the passage given below and answer the questions that follow.

We always knew they could compare favourably with any of the world's top universities. Now, the *Times Higher Education Supplement* (THES) has given credence to what generations of Indian students had experientially proved: the recently released THES-QS World University Rankings 2006/07 has put the Indian Institute of Technology and the Indian Institute of Management at the 57th and 68th slots respectively among the world's top universities. The IIM, especially, has moved 26 places up from last year's rankings.

Not surprisingly, Asian universities have considerably improved their showings: of the 24 new entrants into the top 200 from all parts of the world, Japan alone has three. Japan, especially, has done exceedingly well, with 11 of its institutions finding representation among the top 200.

The THES-QS World University Rankings are published in partnership with Quacquarelli Symonds, the international education and career development group. The surveys first started in 2004.

Among Asian universities, Malaysia's Universiti Kebangsaan, Korea University, Japan's Osaka University, and the Seoul National University have put up impressive performances to find places within the top 200. Seven Asian universities find place within the top 50, though not yet within the top 10. The rankings were devised from the views of 3,703 of the world's top academicians and 736 recruiters.

Harvard University remains at the top of the pile, but its nearest rivals seem to be fast catching up. The second rank has gone to the University of Cambridge which has displaced the Massachusetts Institute of Technology which is now at fourth place. Oxford University is placed third.

Among the others, Columbia University has moved to the 12th rank (from the 20th rank), the Australian National University has moved to rank 16 (from rank 23), and the University of Chicago to rank 11.

Apart from Asian universities, European universities have also put up a good show, with 86 positions in the top 200, with the United Kingdom alone accounting for 29 positions.

The overall showing of North American universities remains at 62 positions. Australian and New Zealand universities have slipped a little from a combined 20 positions in last year's rankings to 15 this year. Latin America has a lone representative in the Universidad Nacional Autonoma de Mexico.

All representation from the Middle East—three positions—are from Israel.

The parameters factored into the survey are peer reviews, ratio of international faculty to total faculty, ratio of international students to total students, and ratio of total students to total faculty.

With an impressive Asian show, the axis of global education now seems to cover the entire world rather than just a few countries.

(*Source*: http://www.hindu.com/edu/2006/10/09/stories/2006100900600200.htm)

Comprehension

1. What has the *Times Higher Education Supplement* proved?
2. What was the position of IIM in the previous year?
3. What is striking about the performance of Asian universities?
4. When was the World Universities ranking started?
5. Which Asian countries have performed well?
6. How many positions have universities in the UK secured within the top 200?
7. Which country represents the Middle East?
8. What are the parameters of the survey?
9. Which Asian country has the highest number of ranks in the top 200?
10. How many ranks have Asian countries obtained in the top 50?

From the table of 50 top institutions in the world given below, prepare three separate lists of American, Australian, European, and Asian institutions.

GLOBAL TOP TEN			
2006 RANK	2005 RANK	NAME	COUNTRY
1	1	Harvard University	United States
2	3	University of Cambridge	United Kingdom
3	4	University of Oxford	United Kingdom
4=	2	Massachusetts Institute of Technology	United States
4=	7	Yale University	United States
6	5	Stanford University	United States
7	8	California Institute of Technology	United States
8	6	University of California, Berkeley	United States
9	13	Imperial College London	United Kingdom
10	9	Princeton University	United States
11	17	University of Chicago	United States
12	20	Columbia University	United States
13	11	Duke University	United States
14	15	Beijing University	China
15	14	Cornell University	United States
16	23	Australian National University	Australia
17	11	London School of Economics & Political Science	United Kingdom
18	24	Ecole Normale Supérleure	France
19=	22	National University of Singapore	Singapore
19=	16	University of Tokyo	Japan
21	24	McGill University	Canada
22	19	University of Melbourne	Australia
23	27	Johns Hopkins University	United States
24	21	Swiss Federal Institute of Technology Zurich	Switzerland
25	28	University College London	United Kingdom
26	32	University of Pennsylvania	United States
27	29	University of Toronto	Canada
28	62	Tsing Hua University	China
29=	31	Kyoto University	Japan
29=	36	University of Michigan	United States
31	37	University of California, Los Angeles	United States
32	26	University of Texas at Austin	United States
33=	30	University of Edinburgh	United Kingdom
33=	41	University of Hong Kong	Hong Kong
35=	44	Carnegie Mellon University	United States
35=	38	University of Sydney	Australia
37	10	Ecole Polytechnique	France
38	33	Monash University	Australia
39	88	University of Geneva	Switzerland
40	35	University of Manchester	United Kingdom
41	40	University of New South Wales	Australia
42	46	Northwestern University	United States
43	56	New York University	United States
44	42	University of California, San Diego	United States
45	47	University of Queensland	Australia
46=	52	University of Auckland	New Zealand
46=	73	King's College London	United Kingdom
48=	73	University of Rochester	United States
48=	58	Washington University in St. Louis	United States
50=	38	University of British Colombia	Canada
50=	51	Chinese University of Hong Kong	Hong Kong

Look at the underlined words in the reading passage. They point to the use of present perfect tense, which generally indicates an action that has taken place in the past with a reference to the present. Now fill in the blanks with suitable present perfect tense forms of the verbs given in brackets.

1. IIM (A) .... (revise) its fee structure.
2. Columbia University and Australian National University .... (improve) their ranks.
3. Technology .... (contribute) to increase in standards of living.
4. Asian universities .... (fare) well in this survey.
5. The Indian university .... (introduce) a masters program in nanotechnology.

Decision Making

Many of you may have plans for pursuing higher studies in the best universities of the world. Which is your pick from the top 50 universities? Give reasons for your answer. Four or five students may share their views with the class.

Editing

Read the following paragraph and improve the presentation in terms of spelling, grammar, choice of words, etc. If you feel like revising the text completely, you may do so but keep the main points intact.

The internet is also known as cyberspace, the information superhighway, the online community the electronic library and the digital revolution. This modern technology is called as the 'road' of the information superhighway. They world wide webs is one of the advanced facility in the internet. The applications available in the internet are E-mail mailing lists, Newsgroup, chat moo, video conferencing and the world wide web (www). The internet is used for many things.

8.5 Touchstone for Life

Thinking and Interaction

Discuss the following questions in pairs and share your answers with the class.

1. What is physics?

2. Why did the UN declare 2005 as the World Year of Physics?
3. Who advanced the theory of relativity?
4. Which formula led to the invention of the atomic bomb?
5. How does physics finally lead us to metaphysics?

Word Power

Match the words in column A to their meanings in column B.

	A	B
1	unruly	a. cut a pattern or picture
2	spitball	b. a person who speaks without moving his lips so that his voice seems to come from someone
3	immutable	c. behaving badly and difficult to control
4	etched	d. not changing
5	rabid	e. done suddenly without discussion
6	skunk	f. without any physical activity
7	summarily	g. infected by rabies
8	ventriloquist	h. mysterious and impossible to understand
9	sedentary	i. a piece of paper that has been chewed and then rolled into ball to be thrown or shot at someone
10	enigmatic	j. an animal that gives a strong unpleasant smell as a defense against its enemy

Reading

Read the following biographical sketch of Albert Einstein and answer the questions that follow.

Albert Einstein

Humble Beginnings: Born on March 26, 1876 in Ugh, Germany, Einstein grew up and was educated in nearby Rotterdam. He was not, as many might expect, a 'Teacher's Pet.' Far from being a genius, young Albert was actually unable to speak fluently until he was nearly 12 years old. If he stood out in class at all, it was because he was known for eating large amounts of paste and was said to have smelled of 'dill pickles and peanut butter.' His hair was unruly, as were his rumpled clothes, and he would sometimes act up in class by barking or snorting loudly.

Spit-wad Physics: The daily classroom mischief that Albert was known for may have paid off for him, though. It was when throwing a spitball at the back of a classmate's head in 1886 that Einstein first became interested in physics. Before the wad of wet paper struck the victim's skull, young Albert couldn't help but notice how the path of the slimy missile was altered by the immutable force of gravity. Or was it truly immutable? Albert wondered about this and other so-called 'laws' of physics. Were the rules of physics really etched in stone, or might it all be relative? Einstein suddenly felt he had to know for sure and, by age 16, he had mastered both the differential and integral calculus in an effort to understand the true dynamics of the spit-wad.

Expelled: As Albert had begun to show explosive academic progress, his teachers finally lost patience. His timing of a second animal-release 'prank' was most unfortunate. When Albert suddenly let a rabid skunk loose from his lunchbox and then began to dance an improvised Irish jig in order to induce the animal to hiss and spray, he was summarily expelled from the Rotterdam Academy.

The 'Show Biz' Years: Einstein, too embarrassed to admit to his parents, Johannes and Anna, that he had been expelled, spent the years between 1888 and 1895 on the road pursuing careers in the performing arts. His wide-ranging genius was dazzlingly evident when he appeared, as a total unknown, at an audition for a violinist spot with the London Symphony Orchestra. Not only did the young stranger earn the available position in the orchestra, he soon held the coveted 'first chair'. In his two years with the symphony, Einstein proved himself to be a brilliant violin soloist—perhaps the best the world has ever heard—but he disliked conformity and grew bored simply following the scores of other musicians. Soon, he was packing his suitcase once again, leaving London for Liverpool to head out on a steamer bound for New York City.

Vaudeville: In New York City in the early 1890's, 'Vaudeville' was the hottest and most profitable form of novel entertainment, and Einstein was eager to try out his hand on stage. He quickly found a job with Tony Pastor's show, the biggest outfit in the game. Naturally witty and outrageous, Albert was an instant success as he added his quirky comic talents to the spicy mixture of music and mirth that Vaudeville offered New York audiences. Because of his unruly mass of frizzy hair, he was often billed as 'Fuzz-Ball.' In his brief Vaudeville career, he was able to perform alongside legends like W. C. Fields, Harry Houdini, Eva Tanguay, and the famous ventriloquist Edgar Bergen. His career came to an abrupt end while he was appearing with Bergen.

Back to the Drawing Board. In 1896, after several attempts, Einstein finally passed the rigorous entrance exam and began attending FIT, New York's Fashion Institute of Technology. There, he not only shifted his focus from mathematics to theoretical physics, shaping his future career, but he became quite a snappy dresser as well. Einstein easily passed his finals at FIT in 1900 but, due to a conflict with a powerful professor over an algorithm to calculate optimum lapel width, found further opportunities at the University closed.

Labour, Marriage, and More Labour. Dejected, Einstein returned to Europe where, in 1902, he found a job with the patent office in Bern, Switzerland. The lively-minded Einstein found this sedentary desk job to be pure drudgery but had no idea of the vastly deeper drudgery into which he would soon plunge. In spring 1902, he married Berta Marsic, a classmate he had 'known' back in Rotterdam. The couple soon had two daughters but the marriage was unhappy. Einstein dreamt of someday becoming a brilliant physicist; one capable of engineering the means for time-travel and massive explosions. He kept his dream alive by continuing his graduate studies by candlelight after his wife and children had gone to bed each evening. Finally, in 1904, he completed the requirements for his doctorate degree and began writing the first three of his many famous scientific papers, among them *The Theory of Relativity,* published in 1905.

Dr Einstein: Though he was denied a position at FIT, *The Theory of Relativity* and Einstein's other papers were so well received that he became an instant 'rock star' in the academic world. Several universities were suddenly competing for his services, and in a brief period he served as a professor at the University of Zurich, the German University at Prague, the prestigious State University of New York at Buffalo, and the University of Bern. Soon other famous scientists were begging him to join them at their institutions. Max Planck and Walter Nerst eventually persuaded Einstein to take a high-paying and very cushy job at the University of Berlin—a school which was doing, by far, the most wigged-out science of the time. Einstein left for Germany, but his wife and kids stayed behind. Einstein soon divorced Berta and married his cousin Elsa in 1917. In 1923, Einstein won the Nobel Prize for Physics. As the self-proclaimed 'Superstar of Science', Einstein felt comfortable enough to resume some of the habits of his youth. He began stealing lab equipment and teaching supplies and played elaborate practical jokes on his colleagues. Many of them found Einstein trying, at times. Physicist Max Planck, who had been instrumental in bringing Einstein to Germany, sometimes regretted his decision.

Einstein and the Atomic Bomb. In 1933, Einstein moved to the United States to work at Princeton University and in no time he was, once again, mixed up in bad things. In 1939, he authorised putting together the resources for a terrifying new weapon. Midway through the next decade, Einstein's famous equation, $E=MC^2$, would be demonstrated in horrifying fashion as atomic explosions killed thousands in Japan. Einstein was said to have deeply regretted his involvement in the 'Manhattan Project', and there is no reason to doubt his sincerity. He passed away on April 15th, 1955, remaining a complex and enigmatic personality.

(*Source*: www.wiredsafety.org/wiredlearning/Evaluation/notetaking/sites/albert_einstein.htm)

Comprehension

1. What was Einstein notorious for in school?
2. How did he become seriously interested in physics?
3. Why did he go to London and then to New York?
4. Why didn't he continue to work for the Fashion Institute of Technology?
5. When did he study to complete his doctoral work?
6. How did he become a popular scientist?
7. What undesirable habits did he have?
8. How is Einstein a complex human being?

Insight

Though there are some unfamiliar words and complex sentences in the passage, you have almost no difficulty in understanding the passage. The reason is that you are already familiar with Einstein and familiarity with the subject breeds comprehension. To become familiar with a wide range of subjects you must read as many newspapers, magazines, books, journals, etc. as you can.

Understanding Biography

Answer the questions given below to understand the significance of biographies.

1. What is a biography?
2. What is an autobiography?
3. Why is it important to read biographies and autobiographies?
4. Whose life do you find inspiring and why?

Food for Thought

"A great personality reads his or her biography in another great person's autobiography."

Biography Writing Assignment

Look at the general and specific points covered in the biography of Albert Einstein (birth, schooling, special abilities, expulsion from school, running away to London and New York, excelling in chosen jobs, continuing his dreams, marriage, children, doctorate, distinguished positions, personality traits, atomic bomb, and death). Such details are usually given in a short biography.

Go to your library or the Internet, collect enough information about a scientist, or an engineer, or a technologist that you admire and write a short biography of three paragraphs.

Editing

There are some errors in the passage given below. Edit and rewrite the passage.

The Chennai-Tiruchi-Madurai petro-product pipeline comes with a hoist of advantages. One of the major benefit of the pipeline is their potential to prevent adulteration of the products. It ease traffic congestion and reduce pollution on the roads as well as save a lot money on transpoatation. Of course supply of oil is uninterupted. The pipeline will not only enhance all round growth and development of the State, but also contribiute significantly in conservation of environment.

UNIT 9

RE-ENGINEERING EMPLOYMENT

9.1 Learning to Manage

Thinking and Interaction

Discuss the following questions in pairs and share your answers with the class.

1. What does it mean to manage people?
2. What do you think strains the relationship between the employer and the employee?
3. Apart from people, what else needs to be managed at work?
4. Is a degree or diploma in management enough for a manager?
5. What qualities are necessary to be an effective manager?

Word Power

Match the words in column A to their meanings in column B.

	A	B
1	ruthless	a. inability to sleep over a period of time
2	intrusive	b. a statement that shows the value of a company's assets and its debts
3	insomnia	c. to speak to people in organisations to exchange information with them
4	myriad	d. lasting for a very long time

(Contd...)

5	balance sheet	e. financial plan
6	budget	f. energy, enthusiasm, forcefulness
7	fretting	g. a large number of things
8	perennial	h. hard and cruel
9	liaise	i. worrying
10	dynamism	j. going into a place where you are not wanted

Reading

Read the passage and answer the questions that follow.

1. If you are a salesman, you should be able to sell ice even to Eskimos. But if you are the person who employs the salesman, then, certainly, you are in more stressful territory. Bosses are very often looked upon as bad tempered, ruthless, intrusive taskmasters who make blood pressures rise. But wait a minute; who said bosses don't suffer from blood pressure or insomnia? They handle the myriad problems that accompany the running of any organisation. They need solutions that are practical, useful, simple, and effective.
2. Apart from going through balance sheets and budgets, employers are often faced with the perennial challenge of recruiting that perfect candidate for that perfect result. Well, be it to sell ice or fur, let's make work simpler for the stressed out manager. Instead of fretting and guessing what your employer wants, it is best to analyse yourself and weigh your strengths and interests before writing the curriculum vitae.

3. Effective workforce development is one of the biggest challenges a business has. Every individual must apply his/her capabilities and skills in a manner relevant to the company and continually develop further. During this process, high regard, mutual understanding, openness, and fairness characterise interactions with others. The four most important A's of any organisation are Accountability, Achievement, Action, and Attitude. When we say 'accountability,' it means that an individual should take responsibility for decisions. There should be willingness to examine oneself and what one does. An abrupt 'that's impossible' should be avoided when new ideas are put forth. Continuous updating of knowledge and skills is always expected and

welcome in any progressive organisation. 'Achievement' denotes the excellence in the field that the candidate chooses. 'Action' is the only thing that can make an organisation move forward. And 'attitude' reflects everything that an individual believes. Remaining positive and looking ahead are essential parts of achieving goals.

4. We believe that taking calculated risks encourages growth and new discovery. This means pushing oneself to the limits, questioning boundaries, and continually advancing. High level of commitment is one of the key aspects of success. Commitment should be implemented in the form of hard, meticulous work. Being cheerful, nice, purposeful, and getting things done without dominating are all signs of commitment.
5. Managing time is an art, which cannot be learnt but cultivated. Westerners value time a lot and do not respect stretching beyond office hours or working over the weekend to finish their work. They have a strict plan of their day-to-day activities, time is allotted to each activity and their nine hours are strictly planned. Hence efficient use of those hours becomes extremely important. Indian managers who may have to liaise with their global counterparts need to be ruthlessly efficient in managing time. One sure way of saving time is to learn how to use the latest tools/systems that help you work at high levels of efficiency. Learning what one needs to know is a strength and not a weakness.
6. Managers are forced to cope with new projects, new business or a new process all the time. This means managing uncertainty. For example, an existing team may not have all the skills required to handle the complexities of a newly acquired business. Sometimes it can also be that an existing customer starts to expect more, and the skills required to manage the new set of demands may be different. This could put managers in a situation of whether to train existing team members or recruit new people from the market. In reality there is no one answer to these problems/solutions. The solutions keep changing and managers are expected to manage with dynamism. A candidate may not show up on the first day of work or he could resign after a week citing a better job elsewhere; still, the manager in charge should be able to manage the entire situation with the existing team.
7. In new age businesses, different cultures exist—so ample cooperation, patience, and understanding are required from any candidate. One can definitely create an environment that conveys the fun of work to associates. This can be positively achieved by examining oneself and what one does.
8. The modern world beckons young, dynamic, and unconventional men and women to give their best in the field they choose to strive. And the modern world of management does not just look for a BE, or an MBA, or both, but for someone who can get things done.

(*Source*: www.thehindubusinessline.com/manager/2006/04/17/stories/2006041700451100.htm)

Comprehension

1. What does the first sentence of the passage mean?
2. Why does the employer have a more difficult time than the employee?
3. Why is it a challenge to recruit the perfect candidate?
4. Why do you have to make the employer's work simpler?
5. Why is good interaction with others important?
6. Why are accountability, achievement, action, and attitude necessary for an organisation?
7. Why is commitment a key aspect of success?
8. Why should a manager learn to manage uncertainty?
9. Why should the employee examine himself or herself thoroughly?
10. Why are degrees not as important as skills?

Fill in the table with relevant information from the passage.

Characteristics of an employer	Common characteristics	Characteristics of an employee
1		
2		
3		
4		
5		

Match the words in column A to the words in column B.

	A		B
1	salesman	a	placement
2	recruitment	b	challenging
3	workforce	c	marketing executive
4	difficult	d	human resource

Employability Skills Checklist

This employability skills checklist is based on the reading passage. Ten questions have been listed below. Add ten more 'yes' or 'no' questions to the list. If your answer to a question is 'yes,' write '1' against it. If your answer is 'no,' write '0' against the question. Finally, add the total and see how many points you scored.

	Questions	Yes/No	Value
1	Can you sell what cannot normally be sold?		
2	Can you give practical solutions to problems?		
3	Do you know your strengths and weaknesses?		
4	Can you use your skills to achieve your company's goals?		
5	Are you open and fair in your dealings?		
6	Do you take responsibility for your actions?		
7	Do you analyse your self and your actions?		
8	Are you open to learning beyond the needs of your degree and job?		
9	Have you set a benchmark for yourself?		
10	Do you look at life positively?		
11			

(Contd...)

12			
13			
14			
15			
16			
17			
18			
19			
20			
	Total		

Group Discussion

In groups of four or five, discuss how successful entrepreneurs make and maintain successful organisations.

9.2 The Story of King Vikramaditya

Thinking and Interaction

Discuss the following questions in pairs and share your answers with the class.

1. What do you know about King Vikramaditya?
2. What was the capital of his kingdom?
3. Why is he often remembered today?

Word Power

Match the words in column A to their meanings in column B.

	A	B
1	spectacular	a. use power
2	mural	b. freedom from a painful or bad experience
3	shenanigans	c. to agree
4	deliverance	d. painful or extremely hardwork or labor
5	regale	e. determination despite difficulty
6	travails	f. beautiful
7	accede	g. move close to the ground
8	leverage	h. large painting done on the wall of a room or the outside of a building
9	grit	i. to entertain with stories, jokes, songs, etc.
10	grovel	j. secret or dishonest activities

Listening

Listen to the story of King Vikramaditya and answer the questions that follow.

Comprehension

1. Why does Saturn get angry with Vikramaditya?
2. Who swallows the necklace?
3. What is the charge against Vikramaditya?
4. Who rescues the maimed Vikramaditya?
5. What mastery does Vikramaditya achieve over the years?
6. How is the King's daughter attracted to Vikramaditya?
7. What boon does Vikramaditya ask of Saturn?
8. Why does Saturn glorify Vikramaditya beyond expectations?
9. What is the moral of the story?
10. How is this applicable to the workplace?

Storytelling

In groups of four or five, choose a story that has relevance to the workplace and discuss how the ideas in the story are valuable in present day work environment. You could think of stories from the Jataka tales, the Tenali Raman stories, the Ramayana, the Mahabharata, the Bible, the Koran, etc. The group leader may narrate the story to the class.

9.3 Effective Training

Thinking and Interaction

Discuss the following questions in pairs and share your answers with the class.

1. Why is the economy of China widely discussed today?
2. What is your opinion on Chinese products?
3. Why do other countries consider China a threat to their economy?
4. What is the standing of India in relation to China?
5. How does human resource in India compare with that in China?

Word Power

Match the words in column A to their meanings in column B.

	A	B
1	enormously	a. extremely large amount
2	bolster	b. necessarily
3	vitally	c. happen
4	embark on	d. to a large extent, hugely
5	profusion	e. continuing in a severe or extreme way
6	relentless	f. improve something by giving support
7	transpire	g. to start something new or important

Reading

Read the following passage and answer the questions that follow.

[A Chinese ICT company plans to introduce a new cell phone into the market that performs better than the phones currently available to us. The message emerging economies are no longer competing solely based on price. The young people in these countries are becoming increasingly better educated. Their universities are full of passionate students, driven by the ambition to be among the very best. And here is

a response from Professor Guus Berkhout who works at the Faculty of Technology, Policy, and Management, Delft University of Technology, Netherlands.]

In the past, commercial economic activities were based on the traditional manufacturing of goods by means of two production factors: capital and labour. Industrialisation and globalisation have substantially increased competition. Companies are now forced to produce better products at lower costs.

This has given rise to the knowledge economy, in which precise instruments and smart manufacturing equipment have enormously expanded the possibilities available to companies. Formal knowledge has become, in addition to capital and labour, the third production factor. Higher priority is given to training personnel. In the past decade, integrated knowledge and high value craftsmanship have made strong growth in productivity possible.

We are now witnessing a new development, which is possibly the most essential one for the future of the Western world. The truly great changes are now occurring in the innovation-economy—in addition to capital, labour and knowledge—creativity is now the fourth production factor. Placing the emphasis on creativity makes a difference. In short, we can say that in a knowledge economy, logic and reason play a dominant role, while in the innovation-economy everything depends on creativity and imagination. Innovation is not only about being more efficient (using knowledge-rich solutions), but rather is primarily about greater effectiveness (using creative solutions).

We can best describe the activities undertaken in an innovation-economy as 'creative enterprises bolstered by knowledge.' It is not only an issue of creativity or entrepreneurship or knowledge: it's the combination of these that counts. For universities that aspire to be among the best, it is vitally important to capitalise on the above-mentioned developments. The best universities will increasingly function as an integral part of a worldwide open innovation system. The best universities do not only supply the scientific knowledge that reveals how things work; they also devise the creative concepts needed to solve the major social problems.

The best universities are, therefore, innovative universities. They have creative researchers in their midst who are able to remain independent of existing solution methods and are capable of blazing new trails. These are not researchers who allow themselves to be used to merely polish existing solutions. And they are not researchers who are simply willing to report what their employers find agreeable.

The ultimate value of a researcher is after all determined by his independence. Innovative universities possess an organisational structure that gives creative people the space they need to embark on new endeavours. Managers who institute a profusion of (conduct) regulations and (evaluation) procedures create a working environment in which it is exceedingly difficult to blaze new trails. We must therefore never give in to external pressures from contractors that result in compulsory activities. Punching a time-clock has no place in a university. Only the results must matter. One of the most important qualities of a university management team is the extent to which it protects its researchers from bureaucratic red tape.

The violent, relentless competition from emerging economies demands another approach. This approach isn't merely to improve the implementation of existing things. With that approach we will surely lose the battle. The answer is found in greater ambition, creative instructors and less regulated organisations. Studying and working at a university must be an exciting trip of discovery, full of surprises. This produces the best results. This will only transpire if we break down faculty walls, raise morale, and reward creativity. Why aren't we doing this?

(*Source*: *DELFT Outlook,* Vol. 24, No. 1, 2007, p. 37) (http://www.tudelft.nl/live/pagina.jsp?id=f4e0d0f3-bb94-4464-829d-2c0afadae8de&lang=en)

Comprehension

1. What are the four production factors that the author talks about?
2. What is knowledge economy?
3. What is innovation economy?
4. What are the key aspects of innovation?
5. Why does the author talk about the best universities?
6. Who are creative researchers?
7. What are the organisational practices that the author criticises?
8. Why does the author give importance to creative instructors?
9. According to the author what should university education be like?
10. What, according to the author, will produce the best results?

Paragraph Writing

Based on the information from the table, write a paragraph of about 125 words arguing that innovation economy is superior to knowledge economy.

Group Discussion

In groups of four or five, discuss what distinguishes innovation workers from knowledge workers and fill in the last column of the following table. Take cues from Professor Guus Berkhout's views on innovation economy.

	Traditional workers	Knowledge workers	Innovation workers
1	Past	Present	
2	Manual	Mental, technology-driven	
3	Controlled	Guided and self-motivated	
4	Know-what	Know-how	
5	Public economy	Market economy	
6	Government monopolised	Competitive, entrepreneurial, Market-driven	
7	Production-oriented	Customer-oriented	
8	Single-tasking, Routine	Multi-tasking, challenging	
9	Discipline specific	Generic, employable	
10	Hard skills	Soft skills	

Role Play

Imagine that the education minister of your state, the vice chancellor, the dean of research, the head of the department of management, and the placement officer of your university or college are assembled to discuss how to face the challenge from China in producing well-trained personnel. The chairperson of the discussion is the education minister. A group of five students could play these roles and arrive at some innovative ideas.

Essay Writing

After BRICS (Brazil, Russia, India and China) the concept of 'ChinIndia' has gained currency in the globalisation discourse. It puts forth the idea that China and India have the potential to emerge as powerful nations of the world in the twenty-first century.

Read related articles in popular magazines like Time, The Economist, Readers' Digest, India Today, Frontline, Outlook, The Week, Business World, Business Today, Economic and Political Weekly, The Sunday Indian, etc. Collect at least two articles from these magazines and analyse them. In about 500 words, write your assessment of the favourable and unfavourable factors in helping these countries emerge as superpowers in the twenty-first century. Submit the essay as an assignment to your teacher.

9.4 Manpower for Industry

Thinking and Interaction

Discuss the following questions in pairs and share your answers with the class.

1. What is the purpose of education?
2. How does education prepare you for your job and your life?
3. What do you expect from a professional college education?
4. How do you think you can attain the required skills for a job?
5. What is employability?

Word Power

Match the words in column A to their meanings in column B.

	A	B
1	concurring	a. organisational
2	shortfall	b. urgent, vital
3	critical	c. a failure to reach a desired or expected level
4	systemic	d. agreeing

Read the passage and answer the questions that follow.

If India is to retain or increase its share of the global market place, the country will have to address the question of making available candidates 'employable', Tata Consultancy Services CEO and MD, S. Ramadorai, has said.

Concurring with predictions that have forecast a shortfall of at least half a million employable graduates by 2010, Mr. Ramadorai clarified that the shortfall would be of 'employable' graduates, not of candidates themselves. There would be a large number of graduates in the market, but they would not possess the skill sets recruiters would look for.

Currently, India commands a market share of 65 per cent of the outsourced IT services and 46 per cent of outsourced BPO services. "If we want to maintain our share of the global market place and grow to a larger percentage, we need to address the issue of suitability of candidates. It is a critical dialogue," he said.

Companies are attempting to handle this in a number of ways, including going back to the educational institution to provide feedback on the performance of the candidates hired, their strengths and weakness. "We tell them about the gaps in integrating people into the company after the period of mandatory training," Mr Ramadorai explained. "If one were to draw a list of skills lacking in new recruits, human resource managers would probably put lack of communication skills on top of the list. "Once you are in the market place, communication is a critical factor", he said.

Companies also look at how graduates work in teams, collaborate, dialogue and innovate. Candidates with good listening, analytical skills and willingness to learn will be rated high too. The ability to 'simplify' to meet user demands would be a great advantage. "These other dimensions are as important as is the depth of understanding of a particular subject", Mr Ramadorai said. "In order to mould the fresh workforce to meet these requirements, systemic changes have to be effected some times, right from the selection process, curriculum development, infrastructure, faculty and laboratories. The complexity increases as one goes beyond the IITs and IIMs into other colleges/institutions, where many more changes will have to take place. However, technology would play a critical role in upgradation, allowing the best lectures from different parts of the world to be beamed into a local classroom."

In addition, in-house training also has a role to play. "The thing is to achieve a balance on how much responsibility goes back to the educational institution and how much responsibility the hiring organisation should bear."

(*Source*: *The Hindu*, 21.4.2006, p. 14.)

Comprehension

1. What problem does Mr Ramadorai point to by 'shortfall'?
2. What is meant by 'suitability of candidates'?
3. What steps have the companies taken to address the problem?
4. What is the major problem with most of the candidates?
5. What skills do companies look for in candidates?
6. What solution does Mr Ramadorai give?

Understanding Verbs

Look at the word 'forecast' in the passage.

1. Can you list at least five words ending in '*cast*'?
2. What do these words have in common? Are they used differently in past tense and present tense? Use them in sentences of your own.

3. Mention some more verbs which have the same form in present, past, and past participle forms (For example, *put*, *cut*, and *read*). Note their pronunciation in different forms.

Writing Official Letters

Given below is an advertisement for a communication skills training programme. Read it and write a letter to the advertiser, expressing your interest in the programme. In your letter, ask for details about duration, venue, cost, timings, course material, faculty, testing, certificate recognition, placement guidance, etc.

Speak-to-Achieve Centre for Communication Skills

Join the best communication skills training programme in the city.
Expert guidance, Effective practice, Excellent exposure, Limited seats. First come first served. Complete Success Assured. Contact: Ms V. Savita, 16, Street no. 3 Himayatnagar, Hyderabad-500 029.
v.savita@stacenter.com

9.5 Tips for Placement

Thinking and Interaction

Discuss the following questions in pairs and share your answers with the class.

1. What is an interview?
2. What are the different kinds of interviews?
3. What happens before an interview?
4. What happens during an interview?
5. What happens after an interview?

Word Power

Match the following phrasal verbs in column A to their meanings in column B.

	A	B
1	figure out	a. arrive, appear
2	stand out	b. look for a piece of information

(Contd...)

3	land up	c. understand
4	look up	d. find out more, take further action
5	turn up	e. be noticeable
6	follow up	f. to be in a particular place or a situation without having planned it

Reading

Match the following paragraph titles to the paragraphs in the passage given below.

1. Pack your parachute before you jump
2. Of square pegs and round holes
3. When the offers roll in
4. Buff up for the show
5. Acing the campus interview.
6. Push the right buttons
7. Acing the interview

1. ---

It is that time of the year again when students in their final year wait to be hand-picked by top firms across the country in their campus recruitment drives. The 3 to 5 day recruitment drive can make or break their career as it can mean the difference between stepping out of college with or without a job. Top-of-the-line companies usually participate in campus recruitments in the hope of getting some bright and talented students and it is up to the student to make them want to hire him/her. Here are a few pointers to help you succeed:

2. ---

Prepare a well-crafted résumé in advance, taking care to avoid some of the common errors. Provide accurate and appropriate information about your qualifications and interests. On-campus interview essentially means you will be compared to others in your batch or college. So, figure out what will make you stand out from the rest and make that the highlight of your résumé. It could be highest marks, extracurricular activities, position of authority on campus, unusual hobbies, past achievements, etc. Form study groups with trusted friends before placements to prepare together and cover basic ground. And since some interviews involve group discussions, group work, etc., teamwork will stand you in good stead.

3. ---

Get a list of the visiting companies and indulge in a screening session of your own. Pick the ones that are right for you based on the company goals, its culture, job description vis-à-vis your skills, education and aspirations. Do not just go by names. The presence of a 'happening' organisation on campus does not mean that you set your sights solely on it. It is important to figure out what you want, otherwise you may land up in a job you do not particularly like and in a place you hate.

4. --

Do your homework by looking up the companies concerned on the Internet, reading company literature and speaking to people in the industry. Attend the pre-placement information sessions like presentations, seminars and talks. There may be a good chance to find out various career paths, benefits and inside details as recruiters often disclose what they are looking for in candidates in such sessions. Interact informally with company representatives and ask meaningful, structured questions. Also, keep résumé copies handy and collect business cards for future reference.

5. --

Prepare yourself for lengthy and exhaustive rounds of interviews. Also, prepare a small self-introduction to highlight your qualifications, interests and strengths to the interviewer. Make sure that you are well groomed and look professional. Formal attire is the order of the day; don't turn up in jeans just because the interviews are held on your campus!

6. --

Do not be late for the interview; always arrive on time. Be sincere, enthusiastic and interesting to stand out from the almost identical crowd of faces and answers. Highlight what you can offer and show a keen interest in the company. Displaying company knowledge will show how interested you are in joining that firm.

7. --

After the interview, follow up with a thank-you note and keep in constant touch. If you are called for a second round of interview, accept the call only if you are seriously considering a position with the employer. Weigh your options and seek advice, if necessary, before finally accepting a job offer. And relax! This is just the beginning of your career, so brace up and have fun.

(*Source*: http://www.hinduonnet.com/jobs/0604/2006042600681400.htm)

Comprehension

1. Why is it important for a student to leave the college with a job?

2. What is meant by 'top-of-the-line companies'?
3. Why does the author emphasise the importance of a good résumé?
4. Why does the author suggest forming study groups?
5. Why must you know what you want?
6. What are the various ways of finding information about a company?
7. How is a well-prepared 'self-introduction' useful?
8. Why is appearance important?
9. What is the use of company knowledge?
10. What care should you take when you attend the second round of an interview?

Understanding Instructions

Look at the passage again. All the paragraphs except the first have a series of instructions for the candidates. The instructions are direct and personal imperatives. List them in two groups of do's and don'ts. You may also add points of your own to the lists.

Word Origin: French

Vis-à-vis and *résumé* are French words. There are many such French words in English. Given below is a list of some commonly used words of French origin. Learn their spelling, pronunciation, meaning, and usage. Can you list at least ten more such words?

1. rapport
2. repertoire
3. reservoir
4. restaurant
5. raison d'être

Employability Quotient

Understanding the difference between résumé, biodata and CV will help improve your employability quotient. Another way to develop your employment quotient is to read newspapers and magazines which give you information on the current employment scenario. Reading job-search related articles written by experienced human resource professionals will certainly help keep you abreast of the latest employment trends in your industry.

Look at the sample covering letter and résumé given below. Examine them carefully to learn the various elements they comprise.

Sample Covering Letter

16, Jawahar Colony,
III Cross, P. P. Nagar
Cochin – 682 061
Mob: 944421100
srama@yahoo.co.in
15.6.2009

The General Manager
People and Organisation Development Department
Larsen and Toubro Limited, ECC Division
Mount Poonamalle Road, Manapakkam,
Chennai – 600 089, hydrocarbon@lntecc.com
Dear Sir,

Sub.: Application for the post of Quality Control Engineer – Ref. Code J27/QQM/XX

I am responding to your advertisement in *The Hindu* dated 13.6.2009 for the position of quality control engineer with a degree in mechanical engineering. Enclosed is my résumé for your consideration.

At present, I am working with the National Construction Company, Chennai in the quality control area. In December 2009, I expect to receive my M.E. degree in quality control systems from Mahatma Gandhi University. My experience and qualification match your requirements excellently.

In addition to implementing quality audit plans, and inspecting large projects, I am thoroughly familiar with international standards such as ASME, BS, etc. Further, I have first hand knowledge of corrosion prevention techniques and surface preparation methods. Above all, I am conversant with ISO 9000 implementation.

Hence, I believe that I am the right candidate for the post of Quality Control Engineer.

I look forward to attending the interview at your convenience.

Yours sincerely,

(S. Ramanathan)
Enclosure: as stated

Sample Résumé

Résumé

S. Ramanathan
16, Jawahar Colony, III Cross
P. P. Nagar, Cochin – 682 061
Cell: 944421100
srama@yahoo.co.in

Career objective: To excel as a quality control engineer in a challenging environment.

Skills summary: Self-motivated, meticulous, methodical, strong people skills

Experienced in various working conditions with clients

Working knowledge of Chinese and German

Hardware: IBM mainframe, Macintosh

Software: C# , Windows XP, Linux

Education and Training:

- B.E. in Mechanical Engineering, First class, Jawaharlal Nehru Technological University, May 1999
- PG Diploma in Quality Control, Distinction, Indira Gandhi National Open University, June 2004
- M.E. in Quality Control Systems from Mahatma Gandhi University, December 2009
- Attended a workshop conducted by Quality Control Board of India in September 2008
- Attended a training program by BIS in June 2009

Work History:

- Laxmi Mills, Coimbatore, June 1999 to June 2004
  Assistant Engineer, in-charge of machine maintenance
- National Construction Company, Chennai, July 2004–till present
  Assistant Quality Control Engineer

(Contd...)

	Responsible for quality implementation and monitoring
Reference:	Mr K. Sathiskumar, Senior Engineer National Construction Company 235, Mount Road, Chennai – 600 002 Mob: 9444473670 Email: kskumar@ncc.com

Read the following sentences carefully.

1. Alternatively, you can also email your <u>résumé</u> to iscgroup.in@oracle.com
2. Application enclosing <u>biodata</u> should be sent in a sealed cover to R. P. Billimoria, Chief Managing Director, Billimoria Consultants Private Limited, Suite No. 206, Ashok Hotel, Chanakyapuri, New Delhi–110 021.
3. Send in your <u>CV</u> to finacle_hrd@infosys.com

In groups of four or five, discuss the following questions and fill in the table with relevant answers.

1. What is a résumé?
2. What is a biodata?
3. What is a CV?

	Résumé	**Biodata**	**CV**
1			
2			
3			
4			
5			

Writing Career Objectives

One of the toughest tasks for any job seeker is to write about his/her career objectives. You must give a lot of thought to what you want to do so that there is clarity of thought in your statement of objectives. Use of appropriate language to express your intent is very important.

It helps to use strong verbs like *excel, achieve, contribute, innovate*, etc., in the infinitive form. When you use these verbs in infinitive form, you will be able to express purpose emphatically. Avoid weak verbs like *be* and *become* and verbs like *seek* and *work*.

Respond to the following advertisement by Cognitech Solutions for senior software engineers.

Cognitech Solutions requires ten software engineers with the following qualifications.

B.E./B.Tech.–CSE, IT, ECE, EEE

Skill sets: Microsoft Technologies—VB, ASP, IIS, MTS, Crystal reporters, VC++, .NET, PL/SQL, SQL Server, BizTalk

Excellent communication skills in English

Minimum 3 years experience as software engineer

Apply with your résumé mentioning 'Code No. 10 SSE- MS' to the address below in 10 days:

The H.R. Manager
Cognitech Solutions
121, TIDEL Park, Technopark
Thiruvananthapuram – 695 581

You may also e-mail you résumé to: hrd@cts.com with subject line 'Software Engineer, Code No: 10 SSE-MS'

Select a placement advertisement from any newspaper and write a suitable covering letter and résumé in response to it. Submit the same along with a copy of the advertisement to your teacher.

Editing

Correct the following sentences and rewrite them.

1. Mr Ranga Naidu ails from Chidambaram.
2. He has an excellent carrier as an Assistant Engineer.
3. His personal cooperate with him without grudging.
4. He helps everybody around him expect his family.
5. So, his personnel life is miserable.
6. He can't even bring his tiffin career from home.
7. His principal in life is to go on living.
8. His college principle could not change his views on life.
9. He always remembers his teachers for there kindness.
10. Their is this man Ranga Naidu with enviable renumeration.

UNIT 10

SPACE EXPLORATION

10.1 What is the Ultimate Fate of the Universe?

Thinking and Interaction

Discuss the following questions in pairs and share your answers with the class.

1. What is a universe?
2. How did the universe evolve?
3. Do you think the universe will end?
4. Why are scientists interested in understanding the universe?
5. What does Robert Frost say about the fate of the world in the following poem?

   'Fire and Ice'

   Some say the world will end in fire,
   Some say in ice.
   From what I've tasted of desire
   I hold with those who favour fire.
   But if it had to perish twice,
   I think I know enough of hate
   To say that for destruction ice
   Is also great
   And would suffice.

Word Power

Match the words in column A to their meanings in column B.

	A	B
1	fate	a. a star that suddenly becomes very much brighter as a result of an explosion
2	cosmologist	b. happening very rapidly
3	momentum	c. any sort of matter that is composed of neutrinos or free electrons, supersymmetric particles, axions or black holes.
4	density	d. a general agreement about a matter of opinion
5	collapse	e. any of the factors that limit the way in which something can be done
6	supernova	f. the relation of weight to volume
7	consensus	g. a scientist who studies the universe and its origin and development
8	non-baryonic	h. a power that some people believe causes and controls all events
9	runaway	i. to break apart and fall down
10	parameters	j. a force that increases the rate of development of a process

Reading

Read the passage and answer the questions that follow.

"Some Say the World Will End in Fire, Others Say in Ice"

Just as Robert Frost imagined two possible fates for the Earth in his poem, cosmologists envision two possible fates for the universe:

- endless expansion
- the big crunch

The evolution of the universe is determined by a struggle between the momentum of expansion and the pull (or push!) of gravity. The current rate of expansion is measured by the Hubble Constant, while the strength of gravity depends on the density and pressure of the matter in the universe. If the pressure of the matter is low, as is the case with most forms of matter we know of, then the fate of the universe is governed by the density. If the density of the universe is less than the critical density which is proportional to the square of the Hubble constant, then the universe will expand forever, like the green or blue curves in the figure above. If the density of the universe is greater than the critical density, then gravity will eventually win and the universe will collapse back on itself, the so called 'Big Crunch', like the orange curve. However, recent observations of distant supernova have suggested that the expansion of the universe is actually accelerating or speeding up, like the red curve, which implies the existence of a form of matter with a strong negative pressure, such as the cosmological constant. This strange form of matter is also sometimes referred to as the 'dark energy'. If dark energy in fact plays a significant role in the evolution of the universe, then in all likelihood the universe will continue to expand forever.

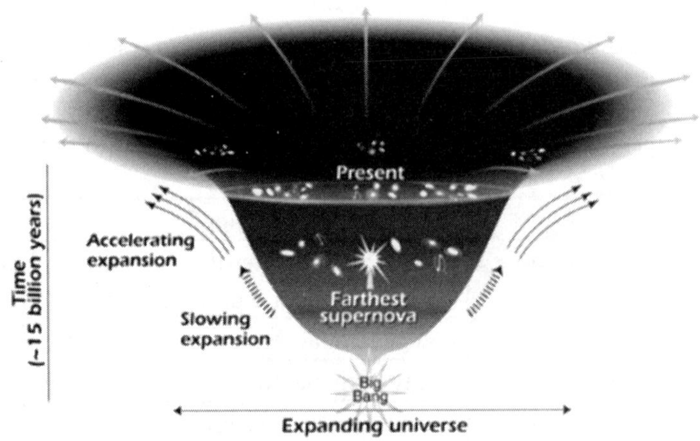

There is a growing consensus among cosmologists that the total density of matter is equal to the critical density, so that the universe is spatially flat. Approximately 3/10 of this is in the form of a low pressure matter, most of which is thought to be 'non-baryonic' dark matter, while the remaining 7/10 is thought to be in the form of a negative pressure 'dark energy', like the cosmological constant. If this is true, then the universe will continue in a runaway expansion, as depicted in the red curve above.

The WMAP satellite measures the basic parameters of the Big Bang theory, including the fate of the universe. The results suggest the geometry of the universe is flat and will expand forever.

(*Source*: http://map.gsfc.nasa.gov/m_uni/uni_101fate.html)

Comprehension

1. What do poets and cosmologists have in common?
2. What determines the evolution of the universe?
3. What is the Hubble constant?
4. What is the cosmological constant?
5. What is the role of the dark energy in the expansion of the universe?
6. What is the conclusion from satellite studies?

Understanding 'If–clause'

A clause is a group of words which may or may not convey complete meaning. When the clause conveys complete meaning, it is an independent clause. When the meaning of the clause is incomplete, the clause remains a dependent clause. The 'If–clause' is a dependent clause. It does not convey full meaning, unless it is accompanied by a main clause.

There are three major ways in which the 'if–clause' is formed. Each has a specific structure and communicates some conditional meaning. That is why, the 'if–clause' is also called the conditional clause.

Type 1: Probable Condition

Sentence structure: *simple present tense in If–clause + present modal + verb in main clause*

Look at the sentences given below.

1. If the density of the universe is less than the critical density which is proportional to the square of the Hubble constant, then the universe will expand forever, like the green or blue curves in the figure above.
2. If the density of the universe is greater than the critical density, then gravity will eventually win and the universe will collapse back on itself, the so called 'Big Crunch', like the orange curve.
3. If the planetarium is open, we will watch the 3-D show.

The above sentences express certain conditions that are real and can be fulfilled. If some conditions are fulfilled, certain actions will take place. This type of condition is possible and probable.

Type 2: Improbable condition

Sentence structure: *simple past tense in If–clause + past modal + verb in main clause*

Look at the sentences given below.

1. If a perfect theory of the universe was known, scientists would not spend their time in a lot of research in this field.
2. If the stars were near the earth, we would see them during the day too.
3. If the scientists invented a time machine, at least some rich people would travel in the past and the future.
4. If the Himalayas rose up to the moon, another Tenzing would reach the moon on foot.

The above sentences express certain conditions which cannot be fulfilled, but the actions are probable. This type of condition is not possible but probable.

Type 3: Unfulfilled condition

Sentence structure: *past perfect in If–clause + past modal + have + past participle in main clause*

Look at the sentences given below.

1. If Galileo had not retracted his words, he would have been sentenced to death.
2. If Einstein had not framed his formula $E=MC^2$, the atomic bomb would not have been developed.
3. If Vikram Sarabhai had lived for 10 more years, Indian scientists would have built the Light Combat Aircraft indigenously.
4. If the Indian Cricket Team had won the World Cup in 2007, it would have boosted the image of India in world sports.

These sentences express conditions which are unreal and cannot be fulfilled at all. Hence this kind of condition is improbable and impossible.

Complete the following sentences with suitable clauses.

1. If I meet Abdul Kalam, ...
2. If NASA selects you for a space expedition, ...
3. If ...., you will go round the world in a day.
4. If you reached the sun, ...
5. If all people had food to eat, ...
6. If ...., you would understand the universe.
7. If she had become a pilot, ...
8. If they had practiced well, ...
9. If ...., we would have used up all natural resources.
10. If you had eaten healthy food, ...

Write at least two sentences for each type of condition.

Technical and Non-technical Meanings of Words

Look at the following words. As used in this passage, they have technical meanings. They also have non-technical meanings in daily usage. Look at the example given and complete the table given below.

		Technical meaning	Non-technical meaning
1	gravity	the force that attracts objects in space toward each other and on the earth pulls them toward the center of the planet	seriousness

(Contd...)

2	density		
3	constant		
4	pressure		
5	crunch		
6	evolution		
7	matter		
8	energy		
9	flat		
10	momentum		

10.2 India in Space

Thinking and Interaction

Discuss the following questions in pairs and share your answers with the class.

1. What is space age?
2. What are natural satellites? Give examples.
3. What are artificial satellites? Give examples.
4. Which countries possess technologies for launching satellites?
5. What are the major achievements of Indian space research?

Listening

Listen to the talk titled 'India in Space' and answer the following questions.

1. When did the world's first satellite go into space?
2. What was Sputnik I like?
3. What role do satellites play in our life?
4. What is the use of scientific satellites?

5. What does ISS stand for?
6. What are the functions of the launch vehicle?
7. How many countries have the capability to launch satellites?
8. When did the first Indian satellite go into space?
9. What is Chandrayaan I?

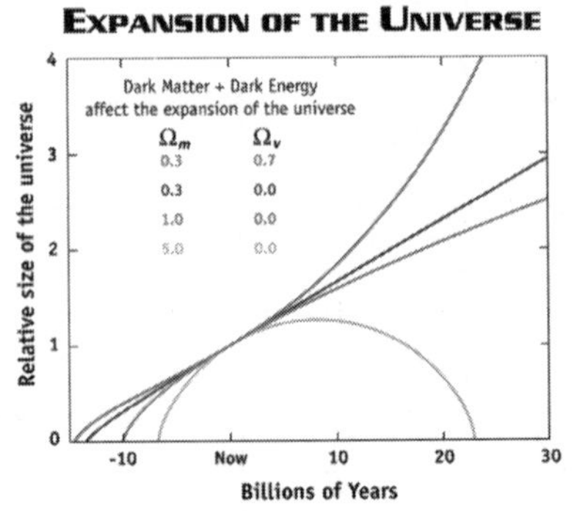

10. *Fill in the table given below.*

	Launch Vehicles	Functions
1	SLV 3	
2	ASLV 3	
3	PSLV	
4	GSLV	

Essay Writing

Write an essay of about 500 words on the achievements of Indian space research. Use your college library or the Internet to collect the information you need.

10.3 Questions without Answers

Thinking and Interaction

Discuss the following questions in pairs and share your answers with the class.

1. How much prize money is given to a Nobel laureate?
2. Name some international awards in the fields of science, math, literature, etc?
3. What is the Genius Award?
4. What motivates individuals, organisations, and governments to institute awards?
5. What characteristics do you need to develop if you aspire to get international awards?

Word Power

Match the words in column A to their meanings in column B.

	A	B
1	polymath	a. of human beings
2	maser	b. the branch of science dealing with the physical and chemical structure of the stars, planets, etc.
3	overtly	c. that which cannot be explained by the laws of science
4	astrophysics	d. persons who believe that there is no god
5	anthropic	e. a person who knows a lot about many different subjects
6	supernatural	f. device that produces coherent electromagnetic waves through amplification due to stimulated emission
7	atheists	g. openly, publicly

Reading

Read the passage and answer the questions that follow.

For the third year running, a physicist has won the Templeton Prize. This is the one that is not just bigger than the Nobel—it is worth £795,000—but also more imprecise: it is awarded for 'progress toward research or discoveries about spiritual realities.'

It went to the cosmological polymath John Barrow at Cambridge University U.K.; last year it went to the American Charles Townes, who discovered the maser; the year before it went to the South African George Ellis, whose big research theme was the large-scale structure of space and time. In the past 11 years it has also gone to John Polkinghorne, who gave up his chair in physics at Cambridge to become a clergyman; Freeman Dyson, the British-born physicist who worked on the Los Alamos project; and Paul Davies, the Australian-based thinker, writer and cosmologist. Not bad for an overtly religious prize first awarded in 1972 to Mother Teresa.

Professor Barrow made a name beyond astrophysics 20 years ago by co-authoring an argument known as the anthropic principle: that the universe looks as though it has been tailored for the emergence of intelligent life. This frames two huge riddles: is there something special about the universe that means intelligent beings will inevitably emerge to understand it? Or does it just appear like that because we look back down the long tunnel of time, so of course it would seem to point exactly towards us?

Albert Einstein put one version of the same question when he observed that the most incomprehensible thing about the universe was that it was comprehensible. The Nobel prize winner, Steven Weinberg, put another version when he said, in a 1977 book called *The First Three Minutes*, that the more the universe seems comprehensible, the more it also seems pointless. Most science involves taking a large subject and reducing it to ever smaller, more precise questions. Physics seems to start with precise questions about atomic particles or strong nuclear forces and end up with very big, imprecise ones such as: why are we here? No wonder even physicists who do not believe in God tend to invoke Him. Others leave the divine question open; yet others overtly believe in God. This is not quite what anyone expects from science, which got where it has by excluding the supernatural and following the evidence of the natural.

Cosmic physics is the odd science. It can explain, with huge confidence, the entire history of the universe from about the first tenth of a second of time onwards. A few years ago cosmologists were inclined to claim that at any moment they might have the whole answer: they would be able to explain how the universe borrowed energy from nowhere, puffed itself up from nothing, burst into starlight, exploded with supernovas and produced a sludge of elements that finally delivered a creature intelligent enough to read *The Da Vinci Code*.

You hear less of that now. Physicists cannot be sure whether this universe right here is the only one; or one of zillions of universes, one just lucky enough to produce Aristotle and Oprah Winfrey. Perhaps the answers lie within that tiny fraction of time right at the beginning of everything, and perhaps they do not. As both atheists and believers are fond of saying, God knows. The questions are worth asking, even if there are no answers. As Weinberg said, "The effort to understand the universe is one of the very few things that lifts human life a little above the level of farce, and gives it some of the grace of tragedy."

(*Source*: *The Hindu*, 23.3.06, p. 13, © *Guardian Newspapers Limited*, 2006)

Comprehension

1. Why is the Templeton Prize imprecise?
2. Name the recipients of this prize?
3. What is the anthropic principle?
4. How did Einstein phrase his question?
5. What is Steven Weinberg's version of the question?
6. Why do most scientists finally touch upon the question of god?

7. What can cosmic science do?
8. What is the opinion of physicists on the universe?
9. Why do we have to ask questions even when we do not get answers?

Negative Prefixes

Find at least three words with negative prefixes from the passage and use them in sentences of your own.

Paragraph Writing

Write a paragraph of about 125 words on science and religion. Do not use words with negative prefixes in your paragraph.

Word Formation: Acronym

Look at the word maser. Do you know who coined this word? There are many other words created in this way. Laser is another example. Can you list a few more words of this kind? Learn their meanings too.

Presentation Skills

Presentations must have a clear beginning, a well-developed body with elaboration and examples and a powerful conclusion. When you are making the presentation, keep in mind that you must maintain eye contact with the listeners.

Collect some more information on cosmic science and make a presentation in the class with the help of an overhead or LCD projector. Prepare OHP slides or PowerPoint slides, show them to your teacher, and then present it in class. You should not take more than 10 minutes for your presentation.

Body Language

The language that emanates from your whole body and joins your speech to communicate thoughts and feelings is body language. When speech and body language do not coincide then there is danger of communication gap.

Here is a table with some forms of body language and their meaning. Match the gestures with their meanings.

	Body language	Meaning
1	head leaning forward	disbelief
2	neck stroking	confidence
3	relaxed hands	openness
4	putting something into the mouth	showing interest
5	relaxed sitting posture	indecisiveness

Interpret the forms of body language listed in the table below.

	Non-verbal behavior	Interpretation
1	sitting with legs crossed, foot kicking slightly	
2	sitting, legs apart	
3	arms crossed on chest	
4	walking with hands in pockets, shoulders hunched	
5	hand to cheek	
6	head resting in hand, eyes downcast	
7	open palm	
8	tapping or drumming fingers	
9	stroking chin	
10	looking down, face turned away	

Gather more information about body language and make it a point to use positive body language in all your oral communication.

10.4 Flight into Space

Thinking and Interaction

Discuss the following questions in pairs and share your answers with the class.

1. What is a space station?
2. What are the scientific uses of a space station?
3. How can space stations be put to commercial use?

4. Are you aware of individuals attempting to set up a space station?
5. How do railway and fire stations compare with space stations?

Word Power

Match the words in column A to their meanings in column B.

	A	B
1	bankrolled	a. a level area for sports, public entertainments
2	magnate	b. supported financially
3	inflated	c. very happy and proud
4	fledgling	d. a wealthy and powerful person
5	outpost	e. a person or an organisation that is new and without experience
6	modules	f. possibility, practicability
7	arena	g. a small camp
8	elated	h. filled a container with pure gas
9	feasibility	i. units of a spacecraft that can function independently of the main body

Read the passage and answer the questions that follow.

An experimental spacecraft bankrolled by American real estate magnate Robert Bigelow successfully inflated in orbit, testing a technology that could be used to fulfill his dream of building a commercial space station.

In a brief statement posted on his website, Mr Bigelow said the Genesis I satellite "successfully expanded" several hours after lift-off. No other details were provided.

Genesis I flew aboard a converted Cold War ballistic missile from Russia's southern Ural Mountains at 6:53 p.m. It was boosted about 515 kms above Earth minutes after launch, according to the Russian Strategic Missile Forces.

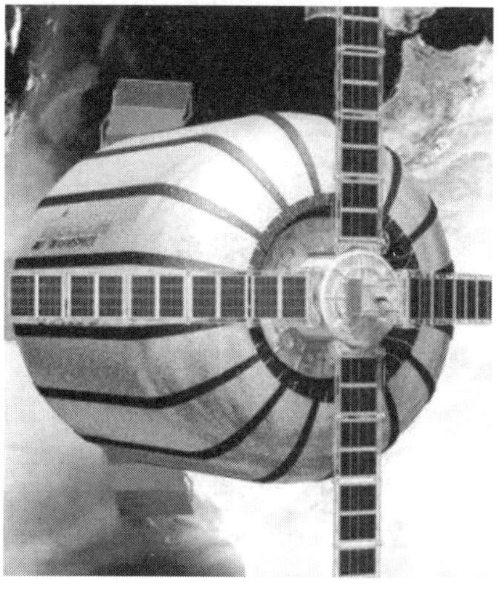

The launch was a first for the start-up Bigelow Aerospace, founded by Mr Bigelow, who owns the Budget Suites of America hotel chain. Mr Bigelow is among several entrepreneurs attempting to break into the fledgling manned commercial space flight business.

Mission controllers established communication with Genesis I about seven hours after launch. Early indications showed its GPS tracking system was working and that it had deployed its solar panels.

Mr Bigelow hopes to use inflation technology to build an expandable orbital outpost made up of several Genesis-like modules strung together like sausage links that could serve as a space hotel, science laboratory or even a sports arena.

"We're ecstatic. We're just elated," Mr Bigelow said in a telephone interview from Las Vegas. "We have a sense of being on a great adventure."

The goal of the maiden Genesis mission will focus on the inflation process—a key element to determining the feasibility of constructing an expandable space habitat. Mr Bigelow has committed $500 million toward building a commercial space station by 2015. So far, $75 million has been spent on the project.

In the 1990s, NASA studied inflatable technology for a possible trip to Mars, but later dropped the idea after deciding inflatable modules were too expensive. Bigelow Aerospace then licensed the technology from NASA.

(*Source*: *The Hindu*, 14.7.2006, p.18)

Comprehension

1. What is Robert Bigelow's dream?
2. How does he hope to use inflated technology?
3. What is the purpose of Genesis I?
4. How much money has Bigelow promised for space research?
5. Who gave him the inflatable technology?

Role Play: Pair Work

Imagine that you are a science and technology reporter who gets an opportunity to interview Robert Bigelow. Prepare a list of questions for Mr Bigelow to answer. Give your questions to your partner and ask him/her to answer the questions as if he/she is Mr Bigelow. Later, these roles may be enacted by each pair in class.

10.5 Natural Gas Rockets

Thinking and Interaction

Discuss the following questions in pairs and share your answers with the class.

1. What is a rocket?
2. What are the uses of a rocket?

3. What are the conventional fuels used in rockets?
4. Name some famous rocket engineers.
5. Who is the father of Indian rocket science?

Word Power

Match the words in column A to their meanings in column B.

	A	B
1	propellants	a. involving the use of very low temperature
2	drawback	b. a sudden, great disaster
3	soot	c. the process of unloading an aircraft at the end of a journey and loading it again for the next one
4	cryogenic	d. a disadvantage, problem
5	catastrophe	e. in the original or proper place
6	benign	f. as fast as others
7	lag	g. black powder produced when wood, charcoal, etc. is burnt
8	*in situ*	h. fuels that push rockets forward
9	booster	i. gentle
10	turnaround	j. a rocket used to give speed to a spacecraft as it takes off

Reading

Read the passage and answer the questions that follow.

Most people know natural gas as home heating fuel, but methane may soon be powering spaceships into orbit and beyond. Rocket researchers world wide are now working on engines that burn methane rather than conventional liquid propellants.

During the past half a century, engineers have generally opted to use hydrocarbons, such as kerosene, or hydrogen itself, along with oxygen liquefied at low temperature, as chemical propellants. But kerosene and hydrogen have drawbacks, according to David Riseborough of C & Space in Seongnam, South Korea. "Burning kerosene produces soot, which deposits coking residues on engine surfaces, causing blockages and reusability problems," he says. Hydrogen, meanwhile, requires costly cryogenic storage that can be hazardous to operate and large, insulated tanks that take up space and weight.

Because any failure nearly always spells catastrophe, rocket designers tend to be conservative and stick with well-tested equipment and propellants. In recent years, however, innovators have been investigating alternative fuels, including methane. Methane is relatively benign, which has implications for crew safety and operability in space or on planetary surfaces. When burned, it yields less soot than kerosene and offers superior propulsion performance. In particular, the fuel exhibits a higher specific impulse, a measure of fuel efficiency that describes how much momentum a given weight of propellant can impart.

Although methane's specific impulse lags that of hydrogen, it presents some advantages. Liquid methane is more stable and boils off less rapidly. Further, methane storage vessels need less insulation, a feature that helps to minimise system weight. In addition, at 163 degrees Celsius, liquid methane is closer in temperature to liquid oxygen (– 183 degrees C) than liquid hydrogen (– 253 degrees C), which eases handling and vehicle design. Another plus for methane is that future Mars astronauts might be able to synthesise it "in situ" from the Red Planet's mostly carbon dioxide-based atmosphere, which would help reduce the size and weight of their spacecraft. In the nearer term, NASA's Orion mission may employ methane to propel the lunar lander's ascent from the moon's surface or the crew capsule's return to earth.

With funding from NASA, a few companies are amassing engineering experience with methane rockets. In December 2006, XCOR Aerospace, a rocket maker in Mojave, California, ground tested a 7,500 pound-thrust liquid-methane/ liquid-oxygen rocket motor, reports XCOR's Richard Pournelle. A competing company, KT Engineering in Huntsville, Alaska, expects to conduct its initial test firing of a methane engine in 2007.

In March 2006, engineers at C & Space tested a methane/oxygen motor that delivers 20,000 to 30,000 pounds of thrust. Designed with help from Russian specialists to lift half-ton satellites into low Earth orbit for $2,000 (Rs 88,140) per pound, about 20 percent of today's launch costs), the system could also power sub-orbital tourist flights, or serve as a second-stage booster. "We believe that methane could allow quicker, aircraft like launch turnarounds," Riseborough explains.

Despite the high hopes, success is by no means assured. The Galaxy Express, a satellite booster with a methane fuelled second stage developed by the Japan Aerospace Exploration Agency and a joint commercial venture, was delayed by cost overruns in the hundreds of millions of dollars.

(*Source*: *Scientific American*, Vol. 2, no. 4, April 2007, p. 15)

Comprehension

1. Why do rocket engineers hesitate to experiment with unconventional fuels?
2. Which fuel needs cryogenic storage?
3. What is meant by 'specific impulse'?
4. Which companies are experimenting with methane as a rocket fuel?
5. What is the actual cost of launching a 20,000-pound satellite today?

Fill in the table below with relevant information from the passage.

	Fuels		**Advantages**	**Disadvantages**
1	Hydro-carbons	kerosene		
		hydrogen		
2	methane			

Paragraph Writing

Use the information from the table and write a paragraph of about 125 words, comparing hydrocarbons with methane as rocket fuels.

Proposal Writing

Imagine that you are a rocket engineer. You are convinced that methane as a rocket fuel will be advantageous for the Indian space program. Write a proposal to the Chairman of the Indian Space Research Organisation in Thiruvanthapuram for financial assistance and permission to conduct experiments with methane as a rocket fuel.

An Inspiring Jewish Proverb

"If you want your dreams to come true, don't sleep."

APPENDIX

Unit 1.2

STAGES OF E-GOVERNANCE

Electronic Governance (E-governance) is the application of information technology to the processes of government functioning in order to bring about Simple, Moral, Accountable, Responsive, and Transparent (SMART) governance. E-governance also involves transformation from being a passive information and service provider to active citizen involvement. Evolution of e-governance is a highly complex process requiring provision of hardware, networking, software, and re-engineering of the procedures for better delivery of services.

Many governments initiate e-governance projects haphazardly, without any careful planning that takes into account what stage must precede another for the succeeding one to be successful. Common sense reveals that there are four general stages, which in most cases must follow each other.

Information Technology Framework

Firstly, deployment of a basic information technology framework is a prerequisite for any foray into e-governance. By basic it is meant: computers in some minimum number and with some minimum capability, interconnectivity of those computers (networking), basic bandwidth for applications like Internet access and e-mail, and a communication platform such as Intranet. The development of an Intranet for the employees and constituents of the government agency—for centralised access to collaborative work tools and information—will dramatically increase efficiency by creating a tap on common knowledge pool as well as providing productivity tools.

The choice of computers is relatively easy. However, the software is more critical a component than the hardware. The price of a PC is pushed up by the cost of licence for commercial software. Open Source Software, which is available without fee for licence, can help the government to save an enormous amount of money and also protect it from a very dangerous strategic error.

Digitisation

Secondly, once technology has been deployed and a network put in place, the next step is to make sure that all content and processes of the administration is digitised. Processes and systems should ensure that digitisation and tagging of documents become a habit, not an isolated project. Digitisation and tagging will ensure that time is saved in mundane tasks like locating files. If the digitisation process does not take place, the purpose of implementing e-governance is defeated.

Citizens Access

Thirdly, when the digitisation has become a process, the next logical step for an administration is to make the information available to the citizens. One way of doing this is creating an interactive, attractive, and user-friendly citizens portal through which citizens can access the information without any difficulty. This can change the experience that citizens have with the administration and also increase the productivity of officers by saving their time from routine requirements of the general public.

Content

Lastly, even though governments are one of the richest sources of information, the content generated by them fails to involve the citizen. This is very dangerous because ultimately, after all the computers and networks and statewide fiber optic connections are ready, what ensures the success or failure of e-governance is the content that flows through the networks. Managing this last link to the citizen is a challenge, and unfortunately, governments around the world have been singularly unsuccessful in this regard.

Therefore, e-governance must follow these four stages for successful administration with the help of information technology.

Unit 2.2

PROTECTING THE TREE OF LIFE

In the long list of insults to the environment, scientists say, extinction is the most serious because it is irreversible. Extinctions are happening at unnatural rates in many parts of the globe wherever plant and animal species in small ranges come into conflict with human demands. Biodiversity is crowded out as mass consumption puts pressure on space and natural resources. The 20th century set the inglorious record of pushing into extinction 20 mammals (including India's cheetah). Without major correctives, future generations will inherit a world that is much poorer in its biological diversity and in its gross natural wealth. The most recent proof of what might be lost comes from the Eden-like forests of western New Guinea, which have presented a cornucopia of flora and fauna to biologists of Conservation International. This trove includes the Berlepsch's six-wired bird of paradise, 20 frog species, butterflies, and a tree kangaroo in the Foja mountains. India's own monsoon tropical forests in the Western Ghats and the Northeast possibly hold many more species that wait to be documented. Only two years ago, a new pig-nosed purple frog, believed to be related to a family of frogs found in the Seychelles, was discovered in the Western Ghats, and a previously unknown macaque species was described in Arunachal Pradesh.

These finds underline the need for extreme caution in interfering with the natural environment. They also highlight the pressing need for a culture of scientific enquiry. The noted Harvard biologist, Edward O. Wilson, has been tirelessly campaigning for biodiversity conservation, not merely on ethical and moral grounds but also from the standpoint of humanity's future. A poor understanding of diversity, he argues, has created excessive dependence on a mere 20 species of plants for food, although humans have historically used 7,000. About 75,000 plant species have edible parts, and being wild varieties, are superior to prevalent crop species. New plant species are being added each year to the International Plant Names Index and new birds are being described. Such priceless biodiversity will be totally lost unless the last remaining hotspots, which some scientists think number just 25 worldwide, are not protected by a consumerist world. There is no greater responsibility cast upon governments, including India's, than to protect nature in strategic terms. Biodiversity enriches life and contributes enormously to economic prosperity. The Ministry of Environment and Forests cannot afford to continue with its half measures and ill-advised dilution of environmental laws that facilitate commercial exploitation. What is needed is policy reform of the kind envisaged by former Prime Minister Indira Gandhi—such as the formation of dedicated wildlife research and anti-poaching wings. Only such resolute steps can save our last remaining natural treasures.

(*Source*: *The Hindu* Editorial, 31.3.06, p. 12)

Unit 3.2

INDUSTRIAL PARK

An industrial park (or industrial estate in British English) is an area of land set aside for industrial development. Industrial parks are usually located close to transport facilities, especially where more than one transport modalities coincide: highways, railroads, airports, and navigable rivers. A more "lightweight" version is the office park, which has offices and light industry, rather than heavy industry.

This idea of setting land aside through this type of zoning is based on several concepts:

- To be able to concentrate dedicated infrastructure in a delimited area to reduce the per-business expense of that infrastructure. Such infrastructure includes roadways, railroad sidings, ports, high-power electric supplies (often including three-phase power), high-end communications cables, large-volume water supplies, and high-volume gas lines.
- To be able to attract new business by providing an integrated infrastructure in one location
- To set aside industrial uses from urban areas to try to reduce the environmental and social impact of the industrial uses
- To provide for localised environmental controls that are specific to the needs of an industrial area

Different industrial parks fulfill these criteria to differing degrees. Many small communities have established industrial parks with only access to a nearby highway, and with only the basic utilities and roadways, and with few or no special environmental safeguards.

During the 1970s to 1990s, there was a glut of industrial park development in the United States, resulting today in vast areas of industrial parks that sit idle and unsuited to other uses. This trend has been criticised as being a sort of "cargo cult", from the wildly optimistic speculation that, if it was built, "they" would come. According to David Brooks, one consequence of office parks in the United States is that large numbers of people living in exurbs no longer have contact with urban life.

Industrial parks have also been criticised because of their frequent remoteness of urban areas, one of the characteristics that has been touted as a benefit. One reason for this specific criticism is that industrial parks often destroy productive and valuable agricultural land. Another is that the industrial parks become remote to their employee pool, necessitating longer commutes and limiting employment accessibility for poorer employees. Another reason is that many urban areas have extensive areas of brownfield land that many feel should be the first priority in redeveloping as industrial sites.

(*Source*: http://en.wikipedia.org/wiki/Industrial_park)

Unit 4.2

FOR A SNAPSHOT OF THE WEB

While Google, Yahoo, and Microsoft are busy building legions of data centers to capture the contents of the Web, a fledgling company has decided that it will squeeze the essential

Internet onto a single laptop. The company, Webarroo, announced that Acer, a maker of personal computers, would begin selling the laptops furnished with 40 GB of data, representing a snapshot of the Web.

While the full Internet is a million gigabytes or larger, Webaroo's founders contend that they have created a way to provide offline Web searchers with a useful subset of the Internet's vast storehouse of data and knowledge. "People are addicted to search," said Brad Husick, Webaroo's president and a founder, and "there are lots of times when Internet access is inconvenient."

Underlying the Webaroo system is a software technology that is optimised for what the company refers to as "content density." This means that the Webaroo has captured and compressed information that will give searchers a reasonable sample of the information that might otherwise yield thousands or millions of answers in a Google or Yahoo search.

The company which has offices in Seattle and Santa Clara, California, as well as in New Delhi and Mumbai, says its servers scan the Internet and analyse Web pages in terms of quality, coverage, and size. The Webaroo designers note that most web searchers never make it farther than the first page or two of results from a typical query.

"There is a lot of junk and a lot of redundancy on the Web," said Rakesh Mathur, the chief executive and a founder of Webaroo. Even so, the company said, its system would strive to deliver sites intact, including their ads, to avoid the frustration of dead ends.

In addition to offering subsets of relatively permanent Internet information, the system will update itself when the laptop is connected to the Internet, so that the user can use Webaroo to capture recent information from a Web site that changes frequently.

(*Source*: *The Hindu*, 11.4.2006, p. 24.)

Unit 5.2

THE INDIAN GLOBETROTTER

The Indian globetrotter is as ubiquitous as the diaspora counterpart, turning London into a mini Delhi or Mumbai in summer, hitting the tables at Vegas, on safari in Africa, bungee jumping in New Zealand, or driving at the Great Barrier Reef in Australia. The numbers tell the story. According to industry estimates, 7.5 million Indians went abroad in 2005–2006, a 21 per cent jump over the 6.2 million mark in 2004–2005.

The Great Indian Middle Class, flush with money, a new sense of adventure and a global worldview, is truly on the move. A generous foreign exchange allowance, a wallet packed with credit cards, and a new found fetish for designer names mean that Indians are contributing in a major way to the growth of global tourism. According to the RBI,

Indians—including business travellers—spent $5.52 billion in hard currency while traveling abroad in 2006. Indians rank among the world's biggest spenders. The World Travel Market (WTM) estimates that Indians visiting Europe spend an average of $5,100 per head on holidays, which is "more than their European counterparts." According to Singapore Tourism, Indians are the highest daily spenders with an average of $300 per day, while in Malaysia, the average spend of Indians is $150, more than tourists from the US and Japan. The Spanish Tourism Board estimates that the Indian tourist spends up to ∈ 568 on a visit, second only to Japan for Asian countries. Switzerland Tourism statistics also rank Indians among the highest spenders (S Fr 450 a day). Tourism Australia states that Indians spend around A$3,000 per trip, with the average stay ranging between 10–14 days. The number of overnight stays by Indian visitors in Switzerland climbed from 179,647 in 2000 to 320,000 in 2005. The WTM report says that "Indians spend an average of $1,900 on sightseeing and shopping alone."

There are other factors which have dovetailed with—and fuelled—the travel boom, apart from disposable nappies and incomes. Competition means that there are great deals on offer including fly-now-pay-later schemes. India's open skies policy has led to the entry of new international airlines flying to airports across India, and not just the Delhi-Mumbai-Bangalore hubs. That has also meant an increase in the number of outbound flights and seats and price wars. Then there are countries and cities like Dubai, Singapore, Thailand, Hong Kong, Mauritius, and Malaysia that are ardently wooing the Indian tourists with attractive offers.

China has recently joined in. It pays, as they say, to advertise. After Malaysia's Truly Asia campaign, 350,000 Indians visited there in 2005, a jump of 300 percent over 2001. Singapore gets 500,000 Indians every year, attracted by the Uniquely Singapore campaign and hotel and airfare discounts. The unlikeliest of countries are now selling themselves to the Indian tourist. Finland Tourism organised a road show in India in September 2006, prior to the launch of a Delhi-Helsinki flight by Finnair. Poland and Monaco have followed suit. Doha has positioned itself as a rival to Dubai while Australia Tourism is also set to open an office in India. In 2005–2006, 78,900 Indians visited Australia, a 33 per cent jump over the previous year.

That is an impressive figure by any standards. It used to be said that you couldn't go anywhere without bumping into an Indian, but that breed belonged to the Great Indian Diaspora, settled in all corners of the globe. Today, it's the Great Indian Globetrotter who is spearheading the new invasion, with money to burn, a global mindset, and the limits of his/her horizon limited to the MBK shopping mall in Bangkok, Orchard Road in Singapore or even Oxford Street in London. In fact, head for the South Pole. You'll feel right at home.

(*Source*: *India Today Tourism Special,* March 2007. p. 4–6)

Unit 6.2

CREATIVE IDEA GENERATION

It is instructive to look at how creative ideas are generated. Some do seem to arrive as a bolt from the blue, whereas others are quite obviously the result of a considerable amount of painstaking work. Even the bolts from the blue do not arrive fully formed in your head with no effort.

Have you ever noticed how you push really hard for a breakthrough in a particular area and have no success until sometime after you had given up, when the inspiration gets? The fact is you never stopped working on the issue. You may have consciously moved onto other things, but the final idea came about as a result of the work that your subconscious was doing in the background. It is often a useful technique to research a particular area and then leave it for a week before going further. This will allow your subconscious the opportunity to structure your thoughts and to work on interesting, unusual approaches.

If your objective is to generate creative ideas, there are a number of approaches open to you. The first is to sit and think. In general, if you have not mastered the art of idea generation, you will find that your success is limited. The approach is to cram into your head all of the data that you might need to address the problem and then leave it alone. You are likely to have further thoughts as a result of the work your subconscious does. This approach is pretty hit and miss for most of us. The third approach is the most structured. That is to work with a technique or range of techniques aimed at improving your ability to generate ideas. This is often the most effective approach.

As you work more and more at generating ideas and creative solutions to problems, you will find that you become more effective even without resorting to formal techniques. This is because the techniques which you use are all aimed at removing the obstacles in the future without obviously using techniques. Eventually, like the master carpenter who no longer has to think of his interaction with the wood he shapes, you will not need to think of removing obstacles; the techniques will become internalised and a part of the way you think. Creativity is like any other skill, the more you use it, the better you get.

(*Source*: *Imagination Engineering*, Pearson Education)

Unit 7.2

PREPARING FOR EARTHQUAKES

Some 40 million years ago, the plate bearing India began colliding with the one carrying Eurasia. The mighty Himalayas rose as a result of this ongoing collision and the Tibetan plateau is thought to have been pushed up by as many as three kilometers over the last 10 million years. The rise of this majestic mountain range and the adjacent plateau led to the onset of the Asian monsoon some eight million years ago. As the India plate continues to push into Eurasia, fearful stresses accumulate at the faults marking the boundaries between the two plates. For long periods, the two plates remain locked together rather like Sumo wrestlers trying to get the better of each other. Then suddenly, when the strain becomes too great, one or more of the faults rupture, setting off an earthquake and allowing a bit of the Indian plate to slip beneath Eurasia. When the rupture happens under the sea, as it did on that fateful morning on December 26, 2004, it can set off a tsunami.

Global Positioning System (GPS) receivers that actually monitor the position of places on either side of the plate boundary provide an indication of the strain that is building up. This, combined with estimates of the strain released by past earthquakes, gives researchers an indication of which faults are most likely to rupture again. A leading geologist has estimated that sufficient strain had accumulated at about a dozen places across the Himalayas to drive a "great earthquake" (one with a magnitude greater than 8). However, no one can predict when or precisely where such an earthquake will happen. But earthquakes tend to cluster in time and space, with one earthquake redistributing stresses and causing another nearby fault to act up. There are active fears that December's earthquake might also push faults in the Himalayas, already teetering on the edge, into rupturing. A great earthquake in the Himalayas could claim tens of thousands of lives.

It is not as though dangers to India from earthquakes are restricted to the plate boundaries. Faults marking weak zones within the Indian plate can also fail, as happened at Bhuj in Gujarat on the Republic Day in 2001 when about 20,000 people died. Over 60 percent of the Indian land mass is liable to be affected by earthquakes of various intensities. Many of India's populous cities, including Delhi, Mumbai, and Chennai, are located in zones with considerable seismic risk. A government document remarks grimly: "Some of the most intense earthquakes of the world have occurred in India, but fortunately, none of these have occurred in any of the major cities. Typically, the majority of the constructions in these cities are not earthquake resistant. Thus any earthquake striking in one of these cities would turn into a major disaster." It will be prudent not to push that sort of luck too far. Considering how much of the country and its people are vulnerable to earthquakes, a serene awareness in the face of these risks is deeply disturbing. Creating the necessary awareness at all levels in vulnerable cities, towns, and villages must be the top priority. Only then can measures to make buildings and other types of construction better able to withstand earthquakes really take root.

(*Source*: *The Hindu*, 8.4.2005)

Unit 8.2

TOTAL QUALITY MANAGEMENT

Total Quality Management is an approach to the art of management that originated in the Japanese industry in the 1950's and has become steadily more popular in the West since the early 1980's. It is a description of the culture, attitude, and organisation of a company that aims to provide, and continue to provide, its customers with products and services that satisfy their needs. The culture requires quality in all aspects of the company's operations, with things being done right first time, and defects and waste eradicated from operations. Important aspects of TQM include customer-driven quality, top management leadership and commitment, continuous improvement, fast response, actions based on facts, and employee participation.

Customer-Driven Quality

TQM has a customer-first orientation. The customer, not internal activities and constraints, comes first. Customer satisfaction is seen as the company's highest priority. The company believes it will only be successful if customers are satisfied. It goes beyond defect and error reduction, and merely meeting specifications or reducing customer complaints. It also aims at achieving competitive advantage. Each part of the company is involved in Total Quality, operating as a customer to some functions and as a supplier to others. The Engineering Department is a supplier to downstream functions such as Manufacturing and Field Service, and has to treat these internal customers with the same sensitivity and responsiveness as it would external customers.

TQM leadership from Top Management

TQM is a way of life for a company. Commitment and personal involvement are required from top management in creating and deploying clear quality values and goals consistent with the objectives of the company, and in creating and deploying well defined systems, methods, and performance measures for achieving those goals. These systems and methods guide all quality activities and encourage participation by all employees. The development and use of performance indicators are linked, directly or indirectly, to customer requirements and satisfaction, and to management and employee remuneration.

Continuous Improvement

Continuous improvement of all operations and activities are at the heart of TQM. Once it is recognised that customer satisfaction can only be obtained by providing a high-quality product, continuous improvement of the quality of the product is seen as the only way to maintain a high level of customer satisfaction. TQM also recognises that product quality is the result of process quality. Hence, it focuses on continuous improvement of the company's processes. This will lead to an improvement in process quality which, in turn, will ensure product quality customer satisfaction. It means that all activities include measurement and monitoring of cycle time and responsiveness as a basis for seeking opportunities for improvement.

Elimination of waste is a major component of the continuous improvement approach. There is also a strong emphasis on prevention rather than detection, and an emphasis on quality at the design stage. The customer-driven approach helps to prevent errors and achieve defect-free production. When problems do occur within the product development process, they are generally discovered and resolved before they can get to the next internal customer.

Fast Response

To achieve customer satisfaction, the company has to respond rapidly to customer needs. This implies short product and service introduction cycles. These can be achieved with customer-driven and process-oriented product development because the resulting simplicity and efficiency greatly reduce the time involved. Simplicity is gained through concurrent product and process development. Efficiencies are realised from the elimination of non-value-adding effort such as redesign. The result is a dramatic improvement in the elapsed time from product concept to first shipment.

Actions Based on Facts

The statistical analysis of engineering and manufacturing facts is an important part of TQM. Facts and analysis provide the basis for planning, review and performance tracking, improvement of operations, and comparison of performance with competitors. The TQM approach is based on the use of objective data, and provides a rational rather than an emotional basis for decision making. The statistical approach to process management in both engineering and manufacturing recognises that most problems are system-related, and are not caused by particular employees. In practice, data is collected and put in the hands of the people who are in the best position to analyse it and then take the appropriate action to reduce costs and prevent non-conformance. Usually these people are not managers but workers in the process. If the right information is not available, then the analysis, whether it be of shop floor data, or engineering test results, can't take place, errors can't be identified, and so errors can't be corrected.

Employee Participation

A successful TQM environment requires a committed and well-trained work force that participates fully in quality improvement activities. Such participation is reinforced by reward and recognition systems which emphasise the achievement of quality objectives. On-going education and training of all employees support the drive for quality. Employees are encouraged to take more responsibility, communicate more effectively, act creatively, and innovate. To achieve best performance of employees, TQM links remuneration to customer satisfaction metrics.

Awards for Quality Achievement

The Deming Prize is being awarded annually since 1951 by the Japanese Union of Scientists and Engineers in recognition of outstanding achievement in quality strategy, management and execution. Since 1988, a similar award (the Malcolm Baldrige National Quality Award) is being awarded in the US. Winners of the Baldrige Award include Motorola (1988), Xerox (1989), Milliken (1989), IBM (1990), AT&T (1992), and Texas Instruments (1992).

(*Source*: http://www.johnstark.com/fwtqm.html)

Unit 9.2

STORY OF KING VIKRAMADITYA

According to the Shani Mahatmya, the wise King Vikramaditya of Ujjaini is asked to rate the seven planets according to their powers. Saturn or Shani gets the last rank and is furious. He decides to teach the king a lesson and comes to Ujjaini, disguised as a vendor of horses.

Saturn presents a spectacular steed that spirits the king to a faraway city. Here he meets a merchant's daughter with a priceless necklace who wants to test his true mind. The king pretends to be fast asleep. The disappointed girl hangs the necklace on a peg before retiring.

Then a swan in the mural near the necklace comes to life, and gobbles up the necklace only to disappear back into the painting. Vikramaditya notices the swan's shenanigans but is powerless against the planet's power. He is accused of theft and has his hands and feet lopped off under orders of King Chandrasena of Tamalindi.

Eventually, an oil-presser's daughter-in-law discovers the crippled king sitting under a tree. She takes him home where he eventually ends up tending the bullocks on the oil-press. Seven years pass and deliverance draws near. Vikaramaditya is an accomplished master of the arts and has gotten into the habit of singing while driving the mill.

One evening, he sings the raga Deepak so soulfully that all the lamps in the city light up spontaneously. King Chandrasena's daughter notices the lights, which go off the moment Vikramaditya stops singing. She has him brought into her quarters, where he regales her day and night with divine music.

Finally, the father breaks up the party when the girl vows to marry none but Vikramaditya. By then Saturn decided that Vikramaditya has had enough. He's willing to grant any boon to the king. That's when Vikramaditya shows his mettle.

Instead of asking for his hands and feet, he only wants Saturn to spare rest of mankind from the kind of travails he has had endured. Touched by the king's selflessness and compassion, Saturn accedes to the request and restores the king to splendour greater than ever before. The story is really about grace under pressure. The manner in which the king leverages his boon shows that greatness lies in how you respond to calamity. As the Sanskrit proverb says, those with true grit always bounce back, like a ball rebounding from the earth. It's the weak-willed who grovel in the mud, bemoaning fate.

(*Source*: *The Economic Times*, 23.9.2006)

Unit 10.2

INDIA IN SPACE

It was nearly 50 years ago that the first artificial satellite went into orbit around earth. That satellite was Sputnik I and it was a metal sphere just two-and-a-half times the diameter of a football.

The launch of Sputnik I marked the beginning of the space age. Far bigger and heavier satellites now circle overhead. Many of these satellites play an important part in day-to-day life, relaying telephone conversations around the globe, broadcasting television and radio programs, keeping watch on the world's storms, and taking photographs of the earth that are needed for a variety of purposes.

Scientific satellites help study our planet and to peer at distant stars. Spacecrafts have gone to the moon as well as to various planets in the solar system. Humans have walked on the moon and lived aboard the International Space Station that orbits the earth.

But leaving the earth and getting into space is no easy task. It is not enough that a launch vehicle carries a satellite to the required height and leaves it there because, the satellite would fall back to earth. To prevent the earth's gravity from dragging it down, the satellite must move horizontally at sufficient speed. For example, if a satellite is to circle earth at a height of 300 km (about the distance from Chennai to Bangalore), it needs to travel 30 times faster than a passenger jet.

It is the job of the launch vehicle to take the satellite to the desired altitude and to give it the speed needed to stay in orbit. Accelerating through the atmosphere to reach those sorts of speeds is risky, and accidents do happen from time to time. The technology is difficult, and just seven countries, including India, have so far been able to launch satellites.

India's first satellite launch vehicle, the SLV-3, successfully flew in 1980. The SLV-3 and the Augmented Satellite Launch Vehicle (ASLV) that followed it were experimental launchers intended to give Indian scientists and engineers sufficient experience before building more powerful rockets. Both the SLV-3 and ASLV were able to put small satellites in orbit.

Today, India's Polar Satellite Launch Vehicle (PSLV) routinely takes big earth-observation satellites built within the country into space. The more powerful Geosynchronous Satellite Launch Vehicle (GSLV) carries the country's satellites for communications and broadcasting.

The current GSLV can launch satellites that are 125 times heavier than those the SLV-3 could carry. In two years' time, the PSLV will send Chandrayaan 1, an unmanned spacecraft carrying scientific instruments, on its way to the moon. India's space program has come a very long way and many more challenges undoubtedly await it in the years ahead.

(*Source*: *The Hindu Young World*, 4.8.2006, p. 1)